CITIES OF AMBITION

BY CHARLES LANDRY

First published by Comedia in the UK in 2015
Copyright © Charles Landry

ISBN: 978-1-908777-05-8

Comedia
The Round, Bournes Green
Near Stroud, GL6 7NL, UK

Special thanks to **Carol Coletta** from the Knight Foundation for
encouragement and insight.
Thanks also to **Lucy Garcia Wordsworth** & **Jonathan Hyams**

Book design: **www.hillsdesign.co.uk**
All photographs: **Charles Landry**

Cover photograph: *In acknowledging Barcelona as the most admired city
the cover shows the Porta Fira Towers by Toyo Ito and b720 Arquitectos.*

This and the other five Comedia publications in this series are available from:
www.charleslandry.com

MIX
From responsible
sources
FSC® C013343

Printed on FSC certified paper, using fully sustainable,
vegetable oil-based inks, power from 100% renewable
resources and waterless printing technology.

Lille: The city has moved from being at the periphery to a hub with its Eurostar station.

CONTENTS

Mannheim: Its annual New Year celebrations bring the city together to plan the future.

THE LANDSCAPE OF AMBITIOUS CITIES

Cities of Ambition is the result of a long term endeavour to understand how cities make the most of their potential and why some cities do more with their tangible and intangible resources than others.

It **summarizes the collective insights**, intelligence and knowledge of insiders, those running cities or contributing to them as business people, politicians, officials, activists and informed outsiders, such as urban advisors, researchers or commentators.

The central messages are: "try to be yourself"; "identify and orchestrate your unique resources"; "be willing to look at things afresh"; "be open to ideas"; "acquire and value the new skills fit for the times, such as being a connector or orchestrator"; "connect across the world and become globally fluent"; "develop a leadership grouping"; and "do not think you can do it on your own - collaborate and partner with others".

Dramatic physical interventions have been made to make the city fit for a world where brain power is more important than machine power. Here people are less mechanical units of production and more the creators of wealth, a wealth that helps to pay for the services citizens need. Surveying the horizon of European urban change and especially de-industrialization over the last 30 years we see how many inauspicious places went from industrial to post-industrial. They generated resonance. They shifted from having a density of resources to a density of networks and circuits where proximity to resources was substituted by proximity to knowledge[1].

This newer city looks, feels and is navigated differently. There is greater emphasis on good urban design and public space, and movement and mobility is easy, convenient, even pleasurable and the benefits of digitization are widely used. The physical infrastructures for an industrial city differ from those of a knowledge intensive city where softer resources, such as places for chance encounter, are as crucial as hardware.

Three overarching strategies have paralleled the vast projects to rebuild transport systems, stations and airports, to seamlessly connect places or to soften the impact of the car or to retrofit old industrial sites or to create new business-oriented districts. The first is being a **'city of culture'**, then a **'city of knowledge'** and increasingly now a **'city of opportunity'**. Today increasingly they are used in unison. The initial step creates the physical conditions to use the city differently. The cultural focus tries to shift the sense of self and identity, the external perception and image of a place, often building new cultural institutions or refurbishing old ones. It is combined mostly with developing the creative industries, such as design, new media or music as well as place activation. Many such cities have subsequently become part of the Unesco Creative Cities Network or a European City of Culture, useful designations that generate pride and they are marketing tools that help a city identify what they are good at and to lure interesting, ambitious and high skilled people to a city.[2] [3]

Three overarching strategies have shaped the trajectory of aspiring cities.

This cultural step led naturally to the second, helping to create a building block upon which cities highlighted their research and knowledge institutions, now increasingly a competitive urban asset which determines whether they can attract good people, organizations and companies. To optimize these knowledge resources that often previously operated in isolation, the triple helix[4] — and now more frequently quadruple helix model[5] — has emerged involving partnerships between universities, business, civil society and public authorities (easier said than done given their diverging cultures). In the third step, cities go on to realize that 'white knight' solutions with big companies solving employment issues very rarely exist and that their key resources are the enthusiasms and dedication of their people who create small and medium-sized enterprises. In the 'city of opportunity', endogenous growth is key which needs a milieu where enabling, agile entities foster connections and provide access to resources, space and skills.

The next steps for ambitious places, what could they be? A few issues spring to mind. This centres on a 360% perspective. What would our cities be like if women had far greater influence on shaping the urban agendas, its built form and the experience of place? Can children, the young and the elderly influence more how our cities should evolve? Living with difference and diversity

Copenhagen: An exhibition at the Danish Architecture Centre.

is a central dilemma of the age. What would an ambitious place do to put this at the centre of their concerns? Will all of this not be beneficial for everyone culturally and economically? Finally, the city communicates through every fibre of its being. Can we create a new green aesthetic that makes it feel desirable and compelling to live sustainable lifestyles?

Ambition & success

Ambition is a significant word. It is a quality that generates energy, motivation and passion from which other possibilities flow. It can jump start processes of change as key people think **'it is not OK to only be OK'**. It precedes vision and is different and more important. It is the pre-condition from which a vision might evolve. It helps people concentrate on both the essentials and the bigger picture and it provides the engine from which commitment grows so that ideas can turn into realities. Ambition needs a purpose and goal. It is not merely about thrusting to be ahead. The aim is for a place to be successful and to provide the scope for its

> Ambition is a quality that generates energy, motivation and passion.

people, organizations and the city as a whole to be the best they can, given their physical, intellectual and cultural assets. This involves choices about what success means. These choices reflect beliefs and attitudes based on value judgements. It involves using politics as well as exerting power and influence to turn these values into policies and projects on the ground.

A successful place is one where its people strive to be contented with their lot, but this requires being alert, somewhat restless and focused seemingly the opposite of contentment. What this means has changed over time and with the *Zeitgeist*. In the past we thought physical infrastructures were the basis of success upon whose foundations economic prosperity could grow. A reliable job and income were mostly seen as enough. Now we realize there is more to success: a sense of anchorage, familiarity and solidity; of possibility, choices and opportunity; of connection, bonds and solidarity where divides between rich and poor are mitigated; a place of caring and welcome where differences can meet; somewhere that provides the ability to self-improve and grow, as well as a sense of inspiration that heightens the registers in our mind. From this contentment grows.

Differing interest groups see success in their own terms and the challenge is to blend these differing aims so they create a bigger whole. The public official may applaud good public services like public transport running on time or efficient garbage collection. Small and large businesses aim for effective logistics networks or light touch rules that give them freedom to act. Activists want to be taken seriously and community groups want to be respected and given a proper role.

Within **a more refined notion of success** economic vigour remains crucial. Yet material well-being is cradled within a set of wider balances blending well the physical, the cultural, economic and social. Urban vitality and viability requires a comprehensive approach. Suddenly being attractive, vibrant, having high quality urban design, good public spaces or a rich cultural life rise in importance. Helping to make this happen can become a virtuous cycle for the public, private and community sectors, as these wider concerns help to generate a better environment for working or to enhance skills, and to create more satisfied citizens or visitors and therefore a loyalty to the place.

Barcelona: The old Casa Battló by Gaudí continues to inspire a new generation of innovators.

The focus here is more on second, third or even fourth tier cities. Usually smaller, they make up the majority of places and house most populations across the world. There is also a concentration on Europe, for two reasons. For many across the world, the distinctive qualities of European urbanity are inspiring. The notions of a shared commons and strong public realm and their way of meshing well public, private and community interests are examples. Also, this is the continent I know best. There are many places in the rest of the world like Vancouver, Melbourne or Medellin and Curitiba that have much to teach and many American cities are ambitious too. One thinks here of Houston, Miami or Seattle that are ambitious in a showy and more conventional way. Others like Portland, Boston, Nashville or Pittsburgh project ambition in their own quirky less showy ways, generally by betting heavily on making great places and highlighting a distinctive local culture. And Chicago manages to do both. The thrusting Asian cities such as Chengdu, Shenzhen or Seoul are hyper-ambitious and dozens more are trying to explode onto the global scene. And in the Middle East, Dubai and Doha are trying to out-do each other with their ambitions to move centre-stage globally. Whether they are liveable is another matter.

... ambitious cities are everywhere, but are they all great.

So much discussion on the global dynamics of cities focuses on the top 20. We know how the **vortex effect acts like a vacuum cleaner sucking up** ambitious, competent, expert people or power brokers into the orbit of global cities like London, Shanghai or New York. These powerhouses, often much bigger, are rolling in an inertia of their own given their intrinsic historic advantages as economic, political or cultural capitals that they can usually maintain into the present. For instance, London would not be so important if it were not home to the global language of English.

... some cities confound expectations, they do far better than you would think.

Many attributes, such as governing a city well, apply to all cities, but some rules cannot apply to mid-ranking cities so the analysis needs to be different. The central question explored here is why some cities with the same resources do better than expected and so **punch above their weight**. What are their features? To discover this we asked: "what are your main reflections and lessons learnt from your years in working in cities?"; "what were the qualities and characteristics that made your city do better than expected?"; "what is your advice to other cities?"; "what are the main future issues cities need to consider?"; "what were the major obstacles you faced?"; and "which cities do you admire?". Some brief illustrations to give a flavour follow.

Pioneers & pathbreakers

We tried to discover why Barcelona is the most admired city (as voted by their peers). From a place 30 years ago people were afraid to visit it has managed to continually be at the forefront of new urban thinking and has practical evidence to show what can be done both in terms of urban design and clever use of new technology. Bilbao equally has been transformed and it is more than merely the Guggenheim effect, as important as the building was. There are many other initiatives and all were based on high quality design of core infrastructure where beauty combines with functionality. Think here of the Calatrava airport, the Foster designed metro or simply its road network. A key lies in its original governance arrangements through Bilbao Metropoli 30, a multi-stakeholder partnership formed 30 years ago, one of the first of its kind. But one must also ask how much does pride in identity (here the Catalan and Basque) account for the determination to do well, similarly seen in the Flanders cities of Antwerp and Ghent.

How did Copenhagen from a state of near bankruptcy in 1993 manage to become one of the world's model cities seen as walkable, liveable and a path breaker? It is a reference point for green city thinking. How did Malmo catapult itself out of mass unemployment and collapsing industries to become regarded as a thriving hub? Key factors include: combining good storytelling about the future with the Øresund bridge linking them to Copenhagen; engaging the construction industry in taking risks to build the carbon neutral Western Harbour, and opening a university that focuses on cross-boundary specialisms like medicine and the environment. These holistic approaches involved **a new form of non-linear planning**, less focused on precise details and more open to allowing conversation and change as plans evolve.

How did Manchester overcome a major IRA bomb, that part destroyed the city centre and use this crisis as an opportunity to rethink its urban core? Why has it been able to receive special treatment and financial possibilities, way above other British cities, and become Britain's test bed for new governance arrangements? Here the stability of political and executive leadership is key. The British government perhaps the most controlling in Western Europe has **infantilized cities and their citizens** who have little control over money and power until the announcement of the Cities Devolution Bill in May 2015. How did Bristol, regarded as one of least effective city governments, use its limited resources

City Highlights

Every city mentioned has a long story to tell of its origins, its reason for being, its high and low points and how in time it has navigated the winds of change. Readers can explore this separately. The boxed city examples have the simple purpose to highlight, in a crisp encapsulation, learning points, common messages, interesting examples of moving forward, catalysts used to jump start development, niches explored, strategic choices made, or how cities tell their story of change.

(yet powerful urban setting) to grow into a city others benchmark themselves against? Having one of the few British mayors may be important, someone who is an urbanist.

How did Eindhoven reinvent itself after Phillips, its major employer and globally recognized company nearly collapsed, so it is now respected by its peers and regularly voted one of the most innovative cities in the world? Its Brainport, with Eindhoven at its heart, has become one of Europe's most prominent high-tech regions. Its social innovations – especially in housing – are also prominent as is its design nous building on the Phillips heritage. Rotterdam, bombed in the war, and one of Europe's most diverse working class cities suffers from the maelstrom effect of Amsterdam. Yet was voted European city of the year by the Academy of Urbanism for its innovative architecture, its housing policies for the city centre and social tolerance, and recommended as a must see destination by the New York Times. It has also left unallocated 3% of its city budget in order to encourage

innovations. Ghent, a historic Flemish city, has built its reputation on its strategic foresight and by reframing its bureaucracy to push horizontal working. Antwerp has managed to become known for more than diamond trading and is now a fashion powerhouse. It has completely revitalized its urban core.

St.Etienne once the weapons manufacturing centre of France and solidly working class has recently been designated to be a creative 'city of design' by Unesco. Here its old craft skills and buildings are being brought into new use. And the small Ostersund, hidden away in mid-Sweden, was voted a creative 'city of gastronomy' based on its organic food production, its reducing food miles strategies and its approach to the hospitality sector. It will host the 40 plus Unesco Creative Cities Network summit in 2016. This is a coup for a tiny place. How did the arctic city Umea attain the prestigious status of European Capital of Culture in 2104 for Sweden against stiff competition? Its forward-looking co-creation approach launched in 2007 is part of the answer as it inspired the international jury. This Northern hub has been a leader in creativity research and has a radical bent with its vegan punk movement being just one of its strange assets.

Why is Helsinki now regarded as the start-up capital of Europe, especially given Nokia's recent decline? Here the city's high class education helps, with the merger of its arts and design, science and technology and economic faculties into a new university called Aalto where cross-boundary working is key. That aside, linking older experienced Nokia brains with young enthusiasts is as important as applying IT knowledge into new areas like gaming and service design.

Mannheim, a city not well-known enough near Frankfurt where the car was invented a long way back, suffers from a downbeat industrial image, whereas Heidelberg, the sugar coated tourist hub nearby, takes the tourism plaudits. But for the young it is different. Mannheim is a music city par excellence where many genres found their German home. It is a unique model for regenerating a declining City neighbourhood, Jungbusch, through music. The sophisticated complex has a high level Pop Academy, creative incubators, and new student housing turning decline into buzz. This is not unlike Essen, part of the famed Ruhr area regeneration, where old factories have been reborn as experience

Mannheim: Ordinary streets also need a touch of inspiration or colour.

centres, workplaces and housing, and where symbolism is used powerfully to blend past, present and future together into a compelling mix. Building innovations focused on sustainable living and fostering the creative industries are part of an overall plan.

Similarly industrial is Lille, a leader in metropolitan governance, where 85 municipalities have joined together to focus on strategic city region issues, such as economic development and planning. They understand that the functional city is distinct from the administrative city and needs to operate in new ways. Surprisingly for France, they bid for the Olympics in 2004 and boosted the perception of the city and enhanced their self-confidence, subsequently winning the European City of Culture award in the same year. This was carried out in the city-region and strongly geared to create a legacy. This reminds us of how important awards can be when used well. Nantes, an important

... every city can make more of their potential.

13

Hamburg: The Elbphilharmonie, an original re-use of an old warehouse in the harbour.

player historically in the industrial revolution, has revitalized its former harbour area, Isle de Nantes, largely through bold artistic initiatives of which the famous wonderfully out-of-scale elephants from *Machines of the Isle* are best known. They are part of the aim to become a "creative metropole of dream and of fantasy". Involved in the slave trade that once made them rich and where 40% of slaves went via the port, they are the only city to acknowledge this dark history through their Memorial to the Abolition of Slavery.

San Sebastian, increasingly successful straddling the French/Spanish border has an unusually clever and successful surfing cluster. Part of their "intelligent research specialization", this uses a unique cultural resource, the surf, which has multiple applications for invention, but is difficult for others to replicate. Another special resource is gastronomy and San Sebastian has the highest density of Michelin-starred restaurants in the world. How did Dublin manage to become the launch pad into Europe for American high tech firms? Then there are Tallinn and Estonia. What was the trigger that made them one of the most connected and digitally advanced cities/countries in the world? Wifi is ubiquitous. A company can be set up in 18 minutes, tax returns filed and completed in a less than a day, foreigners can apply to become e-residents, all personal data is held in Cloud Estonia. The aim in 1989 was get away from Russia as fast as possible and as a country with 1.2 million people it needed to bind itself into a world-wide web of networks.

The list of problems solved is impressive, but no city would claim it has reached its ambition. Precisely the idea of **being on a never ending journey gives them drive** as endemic skills shortages remain, negative images still hold them back, or old mindsets linger.

Ordinary ambition looks like over-ambition for the complacent and less alert. Yet untempered ambition without fine judgement can get people carried away by grandiose plans. People can become trapped in the fatal attraction of the mega project, that once underway is difficult to pull back. The Sochi Olympics 2014 is the extreme example initially budgeted at $12 billion and ending up costing £51 billion for a series of facilities that will remain underused. The costs of the Elbphilharmonie by Herzog de Meuron in Hamburg rose from £240 million to £789 million, but it will at least become a recognizable icon given its brave conception of a concert hall and living quarters built on top of an old warehouse. Add to which it is cradled within the HafenCity, one of the most successful and largest mixed use urban regeneration schemes. Its public realm work is widely acclaimed and its planning is so far-sighted that it has been built to handle predicted sea rises of over one metre over the next 100 years.

The collective endeavour

Many cities reviewed would perhaps say: at our best we can be seen as **a human scale pocket-sized metropolis** with many of the aspirations, facilities and opportunities of a large-scale city, but the intimacy, feeling, sense of community and connectivity of a smaller place. This is an unusual combination.

Successful city making is not a simple job. It cannot be approached in a one-dimensional way. Ambitious places understand how assets work at a deeper level – how you amass them, invest in them, balance them and use them to powerful effect. They accumulate all types of capital and so build wealth creation and social capital simultaneously. **More shallow places think** the trick is simply to amass one alone – finance – and to judge everything on that one criterion believing it ensures efficiency and effectiveness.

Taking an overview of cities we can detect that they are **valuing all forms of capital**, and they nurture, manage and orchestrate this complex of capitals or urban currencies when shaping their future: human capital, the special knowledge of their people; social capital, the complex web of relationships that make up civil society; cultural capital, the sense of belonging and understanding of the unique identity and distinctiveness of a place; creative capital, harnessing the capacity to be curious, to imagine, to be original and inventive; intellectual capital, the analytical capacity of a community; scientific and technical capital, the knowledge base and practical wisdom of a city; democratic capital, the ability of communities to foster a culture of discussion that helps build resilience and future-proofing; environmental capital the built and natural landscape and ecology; heritage capital, the historic resources and traditions of a place which contribute to identity and self-knowledge; leadership capital – the motivation, will, energy and capacity to take responsibility and lead; and finally financial capital – how resources are garnered to pay for services and infrastructure. These assets a city can draw on as 'revenue'.

Then the **city exudes generosity** and gives back to citizens more than it takes. Within this framework individual places will have their own signs or measures that indicate they are being successful. For one city it may be recognition by peers or getting itself on the map, as most famously Bilbao has done. Another might judge inward investment growth or low unemployment rates as the key indicator. Others may be satisfied with being known for buzz and some will assess the satisfaction or happiness of citizens. Yet the combined aim of all these indicators is satisfied citizens, healthy businesses and a well-organized city.

Crucially these ideas are embedded in practical projects, such as the Ebbinge Kwartier experimental zone in Groningen[6], Turin's Biennale Democrazia[7], or St Etienne leading the 12 city Human Cities initiative[8]. They reveal a more forward looking approach to city development.

The repertoire

Retro fitting urban infrastructure is the first visible signal of ambition with, in parallel, a focus on culture, harnessing knowledge assets and creating a start-up culture. See the recent vast new station projects in Ghent, Rotterdam, Antwerp, Tampere, Grenoble and Torino. Consider the public realm initiatives in Malaga, Bordeaux, Barcelona and Bristol or the building of new culture houses in Lille, Bologna, Mannheim or Ghent. Torino is a good example of the repertoire as it relaunched itself on the basis of three strategic plans from the mid-1990s onwards whose focus mirrors progressive cities globally. The first direction in essence was to be a 'city of culture', an immensely successful undertaking, to highlight the city's attractiveness and quality of life. From 1993 to 2014 visitors increased nearly 20-fold (similar to the 20-fold decrease in FIAT's employment) from 600,000 to 11 million. This was to set the platform for the second strategy phase, a 'city of knowledge' to unlock the intellectual resources of the city, such as the Institute of Applied Arts & Design. The final strategy is the 'city of opportunity' and it faces the greatest difficulty given the crippling complexities of Italian bureaucracy and heavy tax burdens – especially personal – that is strangling initiative and the ability to harness its innate entrepreneurial spirit.

Torino: An unusual biennale discussing issues crucial to our future.

City-making is a collective endeavour and not one person's job. Politicians or the urban professions may each claim they are in charge, or business or urban activists could argue they are the city's energetic lifeblood. No one person connects the agendas, ways of thinking, knowledge and skill bases. This is the 21st century challenge for cities and why we highlight **the role of the connector** as perhaps the important urban professional. If no one is responsible, then everyone is to blame for our many ugly, soulless, unworkable cities and our occasional places of delight. Partnering across sectors and boundaries becomes vital to harness their combined capacities and resources. It means acknowledging and respecting the distinct virtues of each. The city government is privileged in 'Cities of Ambition' not because it should be the controller, but because of its role in developing the regulations and incentives regime that frames the context of how others operate. Here the public domain holds the overall public interest in view and issues such as equity and fairness. At its best it is an equal player or a convenor, enabling and creating the conditions for business and community entities to perform well. The private take risks to provide goods and services and the activist organizations, often at the sharp end, bring up the new agendas, such as green issues or new communication models. It is the combination that matters.

The most admired cities

Cities interviewed were asked who they admired most and why, here are the results.

Barcelona is the most admired. It has consistently found ways to stay at the forefront of urban innovation starting initially with its extensive physical transformations associated with the 1992 Olympics, followed by its ability to position itself as a hub for inventiveness culturally, socially and, in terms of IT, with its aim to be the 'mobile world capital'. Most admired is its desire to share and collaborate and to 'innovate for cities' rather than for itself. Just 30 years ago Barcelona was a place few people went to. Yet the Olympic process shone a light on one of the most distinctive places in Europe whose Catalan art nouveau history and aesthetic had followed a different path to most of Europe.

Copenhagen follows and is credited with fostering the urban cycling movement and urban design trends centred on walkability and green consciousness. Its cross-border collaboration with Malmo (especially the bold Øresund bridge linking the two Danish and Swedish cities together) is admired as is its ability to be seen as a global leader in making a somewhat windy and cold place into a beacon of liveability.

Many go for **Malmo** industrial and nearly bankrupt in the 1990s. "Don't expect me to bring old industries, let's dream about the future" noted their mayor Illmar Reepalu who many regard as the long-term catalyst for change. The public administration used its one resource, the sale of its energy company, to move ahead. People admire how it cleverly switched the narrative of the Øresund bridge project from one about cars to sustainable mobility, so kickstarting a focus on clean, green industries. For instance, the insistence of Malmo to launch a new city centre university, rather than on a green field site, helped create an atmosphere of a youthful city, while its focus on cross-disciplinary studies has attracted gifted academics from across Europe.

In **Eindhoven** it is noted how a declining 'Phillips city' was able to re-emerge as a vibrant hub and become a leader in pursuing the triple-helix notion, where the public, privates and university collaborate. Its Brainport notion is a clever device to bring forces together and its focus on design (the Dutch Design Week is held here) has helped shift perceptions. Equally important is its innovative renewal of old Phillips areas like Strijp-S by Trudo into housing, mixed use and incubation centres or its imaginative renewal of poverty stricken Woensel West through a clever scheme whereby students give their time freely to help the underprivileged in exchange for cheap rents. This immensely successful project has transformed a failing school to one of the best in the province.

Freiburg is admired for its long term credentials as perhaps Europe's greenest city and how it used the Chernobyl crisis to create a determined focus on solar-oriented urban planning with laudable results and where now there are more passive houses than in some entire countries. This generated a virtuous cycle to attract skills, research and jobs.

Manchester is mentioned, especially in Britain, for its consistent long term improvement and ability to harness regional capacities. Its strong sense of self has created cultural vibrancy expressed, for instance in music. **Bristol** is praised for having a bi-partisan mayor with a focus on a green agenda and an understanding of urbanity. **Bordeaux's**

comprehensive integration between transport and public space has admirers as has its strength in drawing out the historic assets of the city. **Helsinki** has its strong advocates, who mention how a Northern outpost has become a tech savvy global leader with the ability to reinvent itself post-Nokia as an entrepreneurial city.

The tax exemptions proffered to Irish based artists captured the global imagination and contributed to the buzz of **Dublin**, which has led to many downstream effects from being an entry point for American investors into Europe, to attracting Google to locate its headquarters in the city to its interesting Digital Dublin initiative.

A decade ago **Glasgow** was seen as the forerunner of the use of culture in urban regeneration or **Bilbao** for its courageous move to lure the Guggenheim and its high quality physical infrastructure from the Calatrava airport to the Norman Foster metro system, and the **Emscher/Ruhr** area in Germany for its dramatic use of industrial history and using its environmental degradation as a trigger to develop a green industry.

Of those cities not in our survey it is **Berlin** and **London** that are admired most. It is the opportunity, energy and rich facilities and a sense of being connected to a wider world that attracts. **Amsterdam** has its strong followers for its vibrancy, economic prowess and its ability to attract interesting people across the globe. **Munich** has its advocates given its affluence, (it is home to BMW) vitality and desirability as a location and attraction for students as has **Stockholm**.

This is the central message of cities interviewed repeated endlessly: "if we do not get rid of the silo we are lost and nothing interesting can happen" (Barcelona); "we have to nudge even our own politicians to understand that integrated thinking is the way forward'" (Dublin); "we are small so we must collaborate, that is all we have" (Groningen); "our competitive advantage is that we know everyone and that we try to work together" (Tampere); and "the European City of Culture in Umea was based on co-creation, it allowed us to achieve so much, I just hope it continues now 2014 has finished" (Umea).

Taking a bird's eye view of the vast amounts of information, research, opinions and experiences with cities there are some clear threads and these can be pieced together rather like a story or long narrative. No single person said all of these things, but together they did. One thing is definite: there are few places in which being ambitious is a natural way of life. The reality is that there were struggles to achieve success in all cases and in most it was **difficult to become ambitious**. **Tradition dies hard** especially where places had reputations built perhaps on former assets such as an industry, a resource or set of circumstances. Views and ways of doing things entrench. They become a mindset. And those who are part of a city's former achievements tend to resist change unless they have foresight. Many leaders described how **there were blockers and interests** as well as power struggles and how people and institutions tried to create obstacles, and how many were unable to think in terms of the bigger picture. People often had to be moved on and there was resistance. Often **the change makers struggled**.

THE ARCHETYPE

An ideal ambitious city

An ideal city of ambition has special features, qualities and attributes. They appear here as a simple sequence or model, but reality is never quite like that.

Ambitious places recognize that their context and operating **conditions have changed dramatically**. They conclude that a business as usual approach will not get them to where they want to be and understand that the resources and assets that gave them success will not continue to do so in the future. They appreciate that the attitudes and attributes that made them great in the past may hinder them in the future.

A set of strong values is the best starting point to initiate change.

The **best cities start with values** about what is important to them in the longer term. On this basis they establish principles they are truly committed to, that guide their actions. At its most general these might be about providing opportunities for citizens and fostering sustainable development, yet they must not be too obvious. Statements no-one would disagree with gain little traction so, for instance, the wish to be sustainable needs a compelling narrative attached to it.

Practical places assess their situation honestly and **overcome the power of denial**. They understand their position and seek help from the best experts they can find to analyse their condition and prospects. They realize the nature of the competitive environment around them, they review their resources and how they can be used in the new conditions they have to confront.

They tackle the really difficult problems head-on and **engage with criticism** and can be visibly seen working just where the problem is. They are willing to be unpopular. Ambitious places use crisis as means to re-assess potential and this can help transform problems into opportunities. They are willing to pay a price for things that might not work and accept the costs. They know you cannot win it all.

Bologna: A city with a deep tradition of innovation, but can it be maintained.

They involve the people, organizations and sectors in their city and **listen to their constituencies** and especially **trust their youth** and go with their enthusiasms. The bigger picture view they paint is open so everyone can find a place in it, so creating widespread ownership and commitment. Such a grand picture, a better word than vision, is broad enough to inspire, but narrow enough to enable practical tasks to happen. This develops a mood of success and involvement which is encouraged not as a matter of charity but belief in the collective power of sharing responsibility.

Leaders explain the direction of travel, but with flexibility in the plan so space is opened for dialogue. They are ready to accept other ideas as plans evolve. This fosters a shared sense of identity to allow different voices to thrive. They do not subscribe to the heroic version of urban reinvention and they **build a team and set of networks** around themselves. This establishes a widespread leadership grouping. Together they discuss and identify catalysts and game changers. However, at the beginning a charismatic person can set the transformation process in motion. The subsequent task is to embed the change culture within the leadership groupings that follow.

This provides the confidence to **challenge the accepted canon** and the inevitable inertia in many spheres. Perhaps how the governance structure or the bureaucracy or cultural institutions operate, or perhaps that vested economic interests might only go for the tried and tested. An open and flexible approach is adopted that dares to risk uncertainty or failure, as they know that without experimenting and testing out ideas and projects bigger gains or successes will be more difficult to achieve. They create conditions **where people and organizations can think, plan and act with imagination** and look for possibilities and hidden resources laterally. The atmosphere created means that challenges are seen as opportunities in disguise.

Along the way, by learning from doing, they **rethink the processes and procedures** and so gently persuade using good examples to overcome organizational rigidities. They realize that getting things done involves partnering so all sectors have to rethink how they operate and what their distinctive contribution can be. The **public administration becomes less controlling** and more enabling and the privates understand that fostering the public interest helps them in the longer term so their business-driven energy can combine both profit and public good. Good places find room for community or activist groups and critics to bring ideas and solutions to the joint city-making endeavour.

Copenhagen: 8 House in the new Ørestad neighbourhood by Bjarke Ingels Group (BIG).

To become effective and to show achievements that create confidence the best cities **think big and start small**, as being incremental allows flexibility to be built-in.

Confident cities go with the **grain of their local culture**, they start with themselves and build from that. They learn from good appropriate examples from elsewhere but do not imitate mindlessly. They adapt good practice to their special conditions and thus act out their uniqueness. To distinguish between fads and fashion and deep trends is understood as important, as the trendy can often push in a false direction.

... public bureaucracies become less controlling and more enabling.

Identifying clear new roles and purposes is a major step and strategies and action plans need to be aligned with them. Building a **strong evidence base** to create legitimacy is a vital ingredient in the process of change. Then to outline a step by step action programme incorporating staging posts and early winners starting with easier, cheaper, shorter term initiatives helps prepare for difficult, more expensive longer term projects. This trajectory anchors a paced and purposeful approach that helps gain credibility. This allows time for reflection even though many want to rush. It also requires adopting new measurements for success and failure.

Leading players possess and express passion at times and they show their love for their city, even emotionally. This keeps up energy and motivation and for them their city is a vocation. They are driven because they want to make things happen and so build momentum to both generate energy and to unleash and harness potential. These actors try "to be in it rather than above it" so become directly involved.

Narrating a story that builds emotion plays a part, as does using the past to go into the future. This grows confidence and helps turn negatives around. To be willing to use unorthodox methods for getting issues across or to solve problems is crucial as doing the ordinary well only goes so far. The best go further, they risk and experiment.

These places try to **communicate well with a real simplicity** of message and clarity of purpose and they work with symbols and emblematic initiatives having **identified meaningful catalysts**. This way they are more likely to get buy-in by telling the story in the right way. It also gets the many to own the transformation. In this overall approach they facilitate, stimulate, regulate and enthuse. This means working the connections and networks heavily and instead of exerting power they trade it for enhanced creative influence. They set aside vanity for the many to take part in the glory. The capacity to self-regenerate emerges from this.

All this is only possible if there is strong partnership capacity so ambitious places instigate quadruple helix linkages between the public sectors, the privates, universities and wider communities of interest. This helps convince governments to assist.

Orchestration is the watchword as good city making is complex and needs to bring the disparate elements together and harvesting the benefits of this broad rethinking takes time, a long time.

The City 1.0 2.0 3.0

A simple way to characterize the different post-war urban development phases and ambitions is the sequence of 'The City 1.0', 'The City 2.0' and 'The City 3.0' whereby the different historic cities can be deemed 'The City 0.0'.

*Manchester: Piccadilly Gardens
renewed picture by EDAW for
CABE (the Commission for the
Built Environment).*

The City 1.0

The stereotype of 'The City 1.0' is: Large factories and mass production; the city is seen as a machine; the management and organizational style is hierarchical and top down; structures are siloed, vertical with strong departments, partnership is rare; learning is by rote, urban functions are separated; aesthetics is less important; planning focuses on land-uses; participation is low. Transport is focused on cars. Culture concentrates on traditional forms and institutions. This is the rational, ordered, technically focused and segregated city. It is the hardware focused 'urban engineering paradigm' for city making.

The City 2.0

The industrial emblem of 'The City 2.0' is the science park and high tech industry; its management ethos has flatter structures; partnership working rises in importance; learning systems open out. There is greater awareness of integrating disciplines. Issues are more connected and awareness of urban software and hardware is stronger. Sustainability becomes a mantra. Urban design and the emotional feel becomes a higher priority. The city is made more spectacular. Gleaming glass towers proliferate. Vast retailing, entertainment or cultural centres try to bewitch. The city becomes a canvas and stage

Typical third space to relax, work and socialize in Meet Maurice in Antwerp

for activities. Planning is more consultative and sees the city in a more rounded way and transport redefines itself as mobility and connectivity. Walkability and pedestrian friendly streets grow. Mixed-uses and diversity become more important. Respect for ecology and the creative economy sectors rise and culture becomes a competitive tool. There is more emphasis on distinctiveness, aesthetics, human comfort, and creating a sense of place.

The City 3.0

'The City 3.0' builds on 'City 2.0', but adds a concern to harness the collective imagination and intelligence of citizens in making, shaping and co-creating their city. It is aware of the user-driven digitally enabled city and the smart city agenda searching more for citizen involvement rather than strategies defined by IT corporates. The smart grids and sensors, open participatory and open data platforms and apps for city services are well developed and the 'city of things' emerges as a possibility.

This 'soft urbanism' focuses on the full sensory urban experience. It is for beauty and against blandness. The city is conceived as an organism. It is adaptive to increase its chances to become resilient and they walk the talk on sustainability. Organizationally it is more flexible; horizontal and cross-sector working is the norm. There is a greater tolerance of risk.

The entrepreneurship, creativity and innovation agenda rise in importance. Open innovation systems often drive development processes and there is collaborative competition. Micro-businesses and SMEs have a greater role. The urban form provides cultural and physical environments to encourage creativity. Its industrial emblem is the creative zone or quarter and 'third places' become important, pop up culture is common. Building seamless connectivity and blending the real and the virtual is a priority.

Planning moves away from a land-use focus. It is more integrative bringing together economic, cultural, physical and social concerns. Mixed use is the ethos, partnership and participation the pattern. Eco-thinking is embedded and the intercultural dividend valued.

Culture focuses more on people making their own culture, less as passive consumers and more to enhance their expressive capacities and is performed in more unusual settings.

The City 1.0, 2.0 and 3.0 clearly overlap and mesh, but less ambitious places still display a 1.0 mindset in a world that increasingly operates at 3.0.

http://urbact.eu/

The European URBACT programme has an enormous pool of lessons learnt and information about how cities have developed in the last 15 years, covering themes ranging from abandoned spaces, circular economies, financial engineering, social innovation, urban mobility to city branding and disadvantaged neighbourhoods. Launched in 2002 and now in its third programme (2014-2020) it is the European Union's response to increasing demands for an EU Urban Agenda. To foster the European spirit, initiatives proposed by cities must include a minimum of eight and up to 12 partners from at least three member states. Since 2002 URBACT's first programme started with a focus on exchanging good lessons from urban development by bringing cities together to develop solutions to major urban challenges. It sought to reaffirm the key role cities play in dealing with increasingly complex challenges. It had a budget of 28 milllion euros. The second programme (2007-2013) shifted slightly, emphasizing a need for integrated urban development and social cohesion underscoring sustainable, integrated pragmatic solutions. Its budget was 67.8 million euros. The current programme 'Europe 2020' with access to 96.3 million euros is more experimental and seeks to turn the EU into a "smart, sustainable and inclusive economy, fostering innovation, increasing employment through productivity and growth whilst enhancing social cohesion". These are mutually reinforcing priorities. A flagship initiative for 'smart' is the 'Digital agenda for Europe', 'Resource Efficient Europe' for the second and the 'Agenda for new skills and jobs' for the third. URBACT has involved 181 cities in 29 countries, and 5,000 active participants. URBACT is a significant programme, yet suffers as with all EU projects from bureaucratic complexities and processes.

THE BIGGER PICTURE VIEW

Ambitious cities know they have to be vigilant, aware of deep trends and to have foresight. They detect the common emerging themes and these include: holistic thinking and being able to look at their city through the eyes of children, women, business, the old and their gifted citizens simultaneously.

They have seen the shift to public interest thinking as being too individualistic as that culture only takes you so far. They know **accountancy thinking cannot make great cities**, it is the non-monetary extra that creates that trick. They realize we live in a world of fads. One day it is the smart city, the creative milieu or creative economy, then the clustering imperative or next day the resilient city. They understand how you take the good essence from these ideas. They have worked out what the circuit breakers like mobile phones or the internet have done and how social media platforms like Facebook or Instagram have re-figured communications and what the emerging industries might be, such as clean tech, nano-based products, or using bio-mimicry approaches. They understand what the world feels like in 24/7 mode.

They are not taken in by fashionable buzzwords and catchphrases like 'smart city' and they know the major information providers like IBM, Cisco or Siemens are jumping over themselves to provide services to the new market of cities. The European Living Lab movement has been important here in fostering experimental initiatives that are citizen driven. Urban leaders are places like Helsinki with Forum Virium a leading organization in thinking through citizen empowered urban services by connecting the public sector and business. Cities like Amsterdam, Berlin and Bologna in Europe are at the forefront opening up data about transport, education, health care, and more. Local governments are helping app developers, civil society organizations, and others to find ways to tackle urban problems from managing power use, to finding cheap rents or how crime-ridden neighbourhoods can be avoided. Open data across the globe is a valuable resource in fostering entrepreneurship so contributing to the start-up culture in many cities.

Rotterdam's new market hall is a huge arch housing residential apartments.

Diving into the digital

'So close to Russia, so far from Silicon Valley' yet Tallinn is an innovation hub and regularly scores with Helsinki in the top ranks of the most digital, the most smart or most innovative cities in the world. It is one of the world's most digitally advanced cities based on broadband speed, cost and availability; wireless internet access; technology adoption; government support; tech-education, technology culture and future potential. This is where Skype was invented, free wifi initiated in 2005 and e-governance was launched. Tallinn understands the enormous challenges of the digitally driven economy and have taken conscious steps to prosper in it.

In spite of suffering a massive cyber-attack in 2007 such as the one that hit Sony in 2014, Tallinn and Estonia took that problem to become the West's leading think tank on cyber security. It is positioning its digital strategy to push itself past its geopolitical constraints. Its e-residency programme does not extend physical residency, but allows anyone, worldwide, to establish a business in the country and to transact every aspect of their legal affairs online. Taxes can be paid, documents administered, notaries and intermediaries avoided, through using an electronic signature. In its first week it attracted more than 13,000 subscribers. The aim is to give entrepreneurs abroad a stake in Estonia's future and indirectly increase the 'population' from 1.2 million to several million in the next decade.

This digitally aware milieu and Tallinn's human scale has created the physical and social environment where people can frequently connect, mostly in public places such as coffee houses and this has force fed an IT and app driven innovation process and spin-offs inspired by the original Skype experience[1].

[1]http://www.realclearworld.com/blog/2015/01/estonias_digital_strategy_takes_center_stage_110887.html

> ... cities have life cycles and they rise and fall.

These changes together create a break in continuity and it takes time for new values or management systems, both public and private, to settle. They are stretched and often do not cope. The older paradigms for running things, in more hierarchical formats do not work. Political parties and the political class struggle for legitimacy or are in decline. The 'contract' or alignment between public and private interests needs to be reconfigured. This is the changing world we are in and it has happened quickly.

In this historical stretch **cities have risen and fallen**. They have phases and life cycles. It is difficult to sustain prominence over a long time. Some have moved from underdog to the very hip and trendy like Berlin and here history and the liberation through the falling wall helped. Others like Birmingham were municipal leaders in rethinking city development connecting arts and city development in the 1980s and in how they broke the 'concrete collar' of their main urban motorway. They collaborated, then they renewed education, they were leaders in the creative industries. They peaked, they then became inward looking and lost their collaborative spirit. Let us hope it comes

Recovering embedded capabilities

The problems for Bologna are not bad enough for the city to act urgently. Its stored wealth and good liveability make it a case for graceful decline rather than vibrant ambition. Bologna is largely known for a crucial, globally significant innovation 'the university' a word coined there when it was founded in 1088 and widely considered to be the first. It arose around mutual aid societies of foreign students called "nations" who hired scholars to teach them. The city derived significant revenue from visiting foreign students who developed a strong position of collective bargaining. Something perhaps etched into the city's psyche. With illustrious alumni and faculty through the centuries from Dante Alighieri, Leon Battista Alberti, to Nicolaus Copernicus or Albrecht Dürer and more recently Guglielmo Marconi, Umberto Eco or Pier Paolo Pasolini Bologna inevitably was innovative ranging from medical advances to philosophy.

Emilia Romagna, with Bologna at its heart, has another compelling story as it demonstrates an incredibly contemporary alternative. This was why in the 1970s it was seen as an exceptional model of innovation. It combines the values of civil society and community that led to many social innovations, with the industrial requirements of small firm capitalism so relevant to the start-up culture now seen as the pre-condition of urban success. 50 years of left wing mayors until 1999 largely combining a sense of entrepreneurialism with equality and fairness helped anchor this culture.

Here the tradition of self-employed artisans, account for over 40% of companies with over 90% of these employing fewer than 50 people and with 90,000 manufacturing enterprises the region is one of the most intensively entrepreneurial regions in the world. One person in twelve is self-employed or owns a small business.

Ambition and success derive from a cluster of ideas and practices. It is Bologna's ability to add value to agricultural goods, its mutual aid traditions and its deep cultural knowledge of 'sa che fare' (knowing how it works) that created its economic engine. The ability to take a Ducati motorbike apart and put it together again is part of being a Bolognese and a training ground to become an engineer, who then typically might start a company. It fits the idea of the emerging 'makers movement' and its Fab Labs. Yet ironically this is under threat with the system supports declining. The focus on the knowledge economy has detached thinking and doing when deep knowledge of processes helps advanced manufacturing. Can Bologna recapture the cultural software which ran its economic system? One project, Incredibol, seeks to turn the tide and to foster the attitudes and attributes that made Bologna great[1].

[1] http://www.realclearworld.com/blog/2015/01/estonias_digital_strategy_takes_center_stage_110887.html

back. Bologna in the 70s and 80s was one of the most innovative European cities with good quality officials and renowned for its progressive administration. It inspired the Nordic countries, it pioneered free buses, and in response to youth revolts it started innovative youth projects. These were launched and led by the young themselves within a self-management logic. Its 'Propheta in Patria' project from 1990s, now re-launched as part of 'Incredibol', revealed an effective co-operation culture. But then slowly political foresight declined and the 'Milan Effect' took hold. This bigger city began draining talent, resources and investment from the city and the political class did not know how to respond.

History, place and culture

A city's prospects are shaped by its original reason for being, its location, its natural setting, its resources, its industry and its people. This is history and it matters, it etches itself into the local culture. Manchester sees itself as a leader and derives confidence from having been the world's first industrial city and the associated assets linked to that. Think here of grand municipal statements or gestures of civic pride from learning institutions to galleries and museums, a powerful built structure, old factories and parks. Add to that its contemporary music scene, its football, its media industry. The sense that it has a right to be heard and a place in the world derives from this. An understanding of the longer history gives the patience to play the long game and the sophistication to understand politics. Here history pushes forward rather than holding back and provides the backbone of identity. The same is true for Barcelona, and they both behave on occasion as if it were a nation with a swagger and confidence. A similar story could be told for Glasgow, a forerunner of industrialism facing the emerging Americas, but now geographically at the wrong edge for Asia. Yet it was a forerunner in using arts and culture as triggers for regeneration and from that is has used its knowledge assets to do better than expected.

> Cities are shaped by their origins, history, location, their resources and people.

Nantes is another example facing the world as a port, and its shipbuilding industries involved important craft skills that have played a role in evolving their new advanced manufacturing. Nantes now has a presence on the urban map.

Equally historical roots reflecting strong identity shape how Ghent or Antwerp and Bilbao operate. Old cities with a deep past, but with

an eye to the future and crucially a sense of nationhood, perhaps tinged with a sense of resentment at not being independent. Counterintuitively this creates energy and ambition and a 'we will show you' or 'we can do it here' attitude.

This shapes the determination to be self-reliant and in turn fosters entrepreneurship, visible then and now. Above all, they have accrued sufficient political and financial independence to control their destiny so that any vision they create to inspire their populations is largely in their control to implement. Identity creates strength.

Independence shapes the determination to be self-reliant.

Tallinn responded to its history of Soviet occupation differently and wanted to move from that orbit as dramatically and quickly as possible. It connected globally fast, tested and trialled digital technology. The ambition was to make it unlikely that they could be conquered again.

Invention in your DNA

History can move you forward or hold you back when your main resource, say coal or steel, or your location, say a port, or the technical skills of your people, are less in demand. The innovative energy slowly dissipates and past glories cannot be repeated. So cities live off their past often moving into graceful decline, when they are still rich enough, or worse into distress.

Some by contrast draw strength from their history so letting it shape contemporary vigour. Manchester and Torino are two cases in point. They feel they have innovation in their DNA. Manchester draws confidence from being the world's first industrial city, where civic pride created learning institutions and where the atom was first split, the first stored programme computer was created and where at the University of Manchester Alan Turing did ground breaking research and where in 2004 graphene was invented by two Russians. They say it is the lightest, strongest, thinnest, best heat and electricity conducting material ever discovered with vast potential for applications. Now Manchester is home to the Graphene Institute that is generating investment from across the globe.

Torino, the `laboratory of Italy', so the cliché goes and it has an element of truth as this self-perception gives confidence that Torino can reinvent itself. Once regal and still resplendent in baroque grandeur it is known as 'the cradle of Italian liberty' as here the Italian Risorgimento (resurgence) leading to unification found its base.

Elsewhere in our imagination it is FIAT and a car city suggestive of grey, the smell of petrol fumes. Energy from water from the nearby Alps helped launch FIAT at the dawn of Italian industrialization around 1900 and then others followed like the now relaunched Olivetti or Lavazza making Torino a hub. Employing at its height more than 100,000 workers there are now just 5,000. Emblematic was Lingotto, then the largest factory in Europe with 1 million cubic metres and a futuristic test rack on the roof of the building. It closed in 1982 and, refurbished by Renzo Piano, became a congress and shopping centre with entertainment facilities as well as university teaching rooms. Yet it has lost its lustre.

Its design competence, driven by the automotive industry, gave Torino a strategic position. It was less about style and more about design solutions. Now its skills are being adapted to areas like mobility research and other areas of advanced manufacturing. Torino too is the birthplace for Italian radio, TV and cinema, and is where the first Salone della Mode (fashion exhibition) was held. It played prominent roles in developing the workers' and students' movements as well as participatory theatre. It even launched as unusual Biennale of Democracy. Torino has thus acted as the innovation spur that was taken up elsewhere.

St. Etienne: Their Design Biennale is focused on significant themes of global interest.

Cultural attitudes shape how cities go about their business and this can explain their capacities. They are often insufficiently considered. Tallinn says of itself: "efficiency is our religion" or "we are the model of the Protestant ethic". It even has a legend that says "when you are finished the city will flood, so we always have to keep going". Bristol states: "we have an anti-authoritarian streak, that is healthy and unhealthy, it makes us challenge and try out things." People from Rotterdam might say: "enough of the talk, when do we start" and Tampere citizens: "get on with it, we are practical, we are down to earth". Dublin attributes its strength to its people: "we are small, we don't stand on ceremony, we have a certain cheek, we engage, we are welcoming, we are curious, it is in our DNA, this helps our creativity and this has given us economic opportunities". Even the tiny Stroud, near where I live, has a 100 year track record of alternative thinking, replenishing its gene pool first with William Morris-inspired crafts people and then green activists, a cluster of urbanists and circus professionals.

> Cultural attitudes shape how cities go about their business.

So some cities draw strength from their history and resulting culture and others suffer from heightened expectations. Athens and Rome are prime examples of the latter. Culture can take you forward or hold you back. More inward looking places, for instance, cities in the former Eastern Europe still have top-down approaches to city development even though places like Kosice, PlzeÐ, Zagreb, Skopje and Belgrade have good initiatives in them. Inward looking cities find it difficult to adapt to the new conditions where the ability to link, to partner and to collaborate are key.

Noticeably, significant distinctions become apparent between sea facing cities with their openness versus landlocked cities – and especially capitals –and their desire to control and dominate, like Moscow or Beijing.

The vortex effect

... the pull of great cities is extremely difficult to prevent.

The vortex effect is dramatic and powerful. It acts like a dizzying maelstrom confusing the established order of cities. It transforms the relative prospects of places across the world. Central cities either globally or in their continent or their nation exert a magnetic pull, since they suck up the determined, resourceful, influential and hopeful into their orbit. This makes them increasingly stronger. Thus too at a national level Helsinki is becoming stronger vis-à-vis the rest of Finland; the same is true for Lisbon and thus Oporto, the second city is weakening; and Amsterdam is strengthening against other Dutch cities. The same is true in North America as cities in the 'factory belt' weaken (think here of Baltimore, Detroit or Cincinnati) against the pull of places like San Francisco, Washington DC and Los Angeles. The main headquarters of business, research and politics increasingly agglomerate, as do tacit and explicit knowledge, and in a self-reinforcing process **this makes the strong stronger and the weak weaker**. Critical mass accumulates and solidifies as do network linkages, and the gap between first tier cities and the rest is growing and accelerating as they monopolize opportunities and impede the spread of benefits.

Only a few places have counteracted these forceful vortex dynamics. It requires a city region perspective. Most notably Malmo and Copenhagen magnified their capacities and global resonance by connecting the two cities in two countries across the Øresund bridge and overcame numerous challenges to create positive

Berlin: Great art gives cities resonance. Nefertiti housed in the Altes Museum.

synergy effects in trade. Mannheim, the centre of the Rhein-Neckar Metropole, on the other hand, has had greater difficulties as the nearby historic university city Heidelberg does not want to cede primacy to the ex-industrial Mannheim. A simple look at the map reveals how inextricably interwoven the interdependencies and potential are, economically, culturally and socially. Meanwhile, their proximity to and excellent connections with Frankfurt could make the region an interestingly diverse powerhouse.

The greatest pull is exerted by the few first tier cities, like New York, London or increasingly Shanghai or Beijing or even Berlin, that have become strategic places and communications nodal points, which have a direct effect and influence on world affairs economically, culturally and politically, where global agendas and trends are created, facilitated and enacted. Here, cost of living is rocketing sky high, luxury consumption growing, the arts world booming and divisions between rich and poor widening.

... strategic places have a direct effect and influence on world affairs economically, culturally and politically.

Typically first tier places are centres of national and international trade, political power, banking, insurance and related financial services, advanced professional activity of all kinds (medicine, law, higher education, technology, research), information gathering and diffusion, knowledge creation and inventiveness, culture, creativity and entertainment and even conspicuous consumption. They are places with excellent physical and other infrastructures and a stimulating milieu through which money, workers, information and commodities flow. They link economic relations between surrounding regions and the global economy, helped by powerful media outlets with international scope, and they are the base for large foreign businesses and corporate headquarters.

Second tier cities tend to either be capitals of nations with less power or have a cluster of strong global niches like Los Angeles and film or they are secondary cities in big nations. They are well-connected, well recognized and players on the global stage. For example, Chicago, Los Angeles and Frankfurt are significant global cities in terms of economic activities, but less in terms of political power. There are other cities frequently placed in the second tier of global cities, including Hong Kong, Singapore, Miami or Toronto.

Punching below your weight

My first interview with a Flemish person years ago surprised me: "Remember we are self-critical". So no surprise Antwerp says of itself, perhaps a true sign of ambition: "Antwerp boxes not above its weight, but just below its weight and is a city of underutilized possibilities". It likes to define itself as `a restless city', a city that wants to be a-typical so encouraging experiment and innovation. "A-typical is our DNA". The prospect of shaping a place makes it interesting to differing target groups, from students, to entrepreneurs, residents or investors, since the city wants to attract talent, hold purchasing power, and anchor business.

Antwerp is generating contemporary urbanity with a touch of verve, and between 2000 and 2014 Antwerp changed enormously, and this is well-orchestrated through communication and branding that is creating a virtuous cycle. Antwerp's flexible big "A" is the symbol and is used in multi-faceted ways and helps the 'A-typical' message.

Antwerp is more than diamonds and its recent fashion fame. It encapsulates well the European experience where cities update physical infrastructure, use good urban designers, re-create public space, develop parks, give a facelift to their urban heart and shabby areas, build new landmarks, and then in parallel link this to an active cultural and entrepreneurship strategy combining new institutions with a creative economy focus and clustering. The latter is anchored by the Museum aan de Stroom (Museum at the Stream) and the Red Star Line Museum. Further afield a main arts centre, De Singel, perhaps over engineered was expanded. Old buildings like their military hospital have re-emerged within a 'green quarter' where there are top culinary experiences. The city helped buy back dilapidated buildings, giving chances to young architects to renovate abandoned houses, and extended their city core with a mixed use neighbourhood, Cadix, on the docklands. Its ambitions continue. It is refitting older spaces, such as a new eco innovative industrial zone, Blue Gate Antwerp. There is also an Antwerp Expo and tech centres for advanced manufacturing.

The emphasis now is more on the software. As the physical projects that helped create a sense of momentum complete, an emerging buzz has helped increase the tertiary student population dramatically from 30,000 to 46,000 and new facilities like the recently completed Start Up Village in the city centre, with an affordable incubator become increasingly important.

Third tier cities typically fall behind the second tier on every criterion, but they nevertheless remain globally significant given the activities they house. This includes places such as Vancouver, Sydney, Munich, Milan and Rio de Janeiro, each having something special to offer the world, be it a specialist industry, a lifestyle, fashion or cultural vibrancy.

... every place has chances to become a hub.

A fourth tier city can be of considerable size with the associated economic activities attached, but it falls outside of the main pathway of global connections and exchange, even though it might have strong specialisms. These cities can be known to the cognoscenti and might be a niche tourism destination, but they are always fighting for acknowledgement. Such places usually look to others as leaders and trendsetters, but the best find niches to give them prominence or are simply good at being themselves.

Creating centrality

Transport is "the maker and breaker of cities" and connectivity is key so fierce battles ensue to be a turntable for urban movement systems. Rail infrastructure is again in vogue. It is more time effective, with comfortable moving offices, than car or air for journeys up to 500km, especially with the convenience of city centre to centre access.

Cities historically faded when railways or airports passed them by and can disappear from our consciousness when not on transport maps. Good public transport can foreshorten the perception of distance and given its speed and ease of access also shift mental geography. Places feel closer. Dusseldorf is on the radar screen and is better known than Dortmund or Essen, all cities with the same size, who use the airport called Dusseldorf. This has downstream effects.

Being a hub can have dramatic effects as can speeding up time through high speed rail. They provide impetus for growth. Lille once seen as a northern industrial outpost at the edge of France overnight through Eurostar became a core destination between London, Paris and Brussels. This is why the mayor Pierre Mauroy fought tenaciously to literally put Lille on the map. This was the primary catalyst that allowed first the French and then foreigners to discover that the Lille metropolitan region was more than coal and a city of substance.

The Milan/Torino journey until recently took two hours. With fast rail it has reduced to 40 minutes transforming transaction capacities and force feeding opportunities and linkage. Suddenly two large cities have become a metro-region. Dutch train connectivity across the Randstad is renowned and it is possible to live in Rotterdam, work in Amsterdam and have meeting in The Hague all in a day.[1]

[1] http://www.jstor.org/discover/10.2307/40101624?sid=21106386802153&uid=373 8032&uid=4&uid=2

Company cities to start-up cities

Eindhoven will always be associated with Phillips, Torino with Fiat, and Helsinki with Nokia. Yet the era of one-company cities is ending. The experience and sophisticated skills to run global companies or complex supply chains to make these operations work embody vast reservoirs of often unseen skills. Yet if conditions are right they can be the seedbed for relaunching a city's economy through medium and smaller companies. All three cities have focused on providing the space, skills, finance and support systems to foster the rise of a start-up culture.

Note how large tech organisations from Silicon Valley and China have moved their R&D facilities to Finland in a bid to draw on the expertise of ex-Nokia employees which alone in Helsinki region were 10,000. These experienced managers have been part of the underbelly of the Finnish start-up revolution either as key staff or business angels. These older heads have played a part in helping the young teams at Rovio (Angry Birds) or Supercell (Clash of Clans) as IT knowledge switched into the gaming industry. The latter have been a major players in launching Slush Europe's largest start-up event.

Equally ex-Phillips employees in Eindhoven, have made the city according to Forbes "hands-down the most inventive city in the world" based on one of the most commonly used metrics for mapping the geography of innovation called "patent intensity.". Think here beyond Phillips (now involved in healthcare as well as lighting and consumer lifestyles) of NXP, ASML, and Oce. See here how Torino's applied design skills that attracted the automotive components industry are finding new applications elsewhere for instance sustainable mobility.

The Metropolis: A perspective

Place attachment is strong, yet the metropolitan view is increasingly vital. but it remains problematic and contradictory. It has not always worked well when voters in the outer suburbs with less interest in the urban core shape a city's prospects negatively. Yet at the same time issues like public transport or economic development cannot be assessed at the very local level. Toronto here is an example of the dilemmas. In the positive cases where metro thinking works the smaller locales have their roles acknowledged and they in turn accept the primary role of the core city.

This is why Howard Bernstein, the CEO of Manchester can say: "My main advice to others is to focus on place rather than institutional boundaries" that is "why we voted to have a combined authority across 10 municipalities". Other good examples include Lille which created the concept of Lille Metropole and reconfigured its centrality by becoming a major stop for the Eurostar, thus placing it at the centre of a triangle linking Paris, London and Brussels. This required intense lobbying, building an evidence base, and exploiting the connections and networking capacity of former mayor Pierre Mauroy (being an ex-French prime minister helped). Crucially it meant enticing disparate groups by setting out claims

for a bigger, more important Lille. The 85 smaller surrounding localities like Roubaix could clearly see the benefits. Emscher Park and the Ruhr underwent a similar process to create a significant metropolis, although here the centrifugal pull is powerful. Ghent and Antwerp as Flanders in effect operate regionally.

The Randstad metropolitan region, a swathe of places encompassing Amsterdam, The Hague, Rotterdam and Utrecht in western Netherlands, is regarded worldwide as a model of a successful polycentric metropolis. This networked cluster of cities works, but by contrast is more controversial mainly in terms of who benefits. Is it the vortex effect of Amsterdam, as most now claim, with the others playing subsidiary roles?

Place carries with it many emotions and its loyalties are mostly very local. It comes in myriad forms like football. Take Turin with Juventus and FC Torino or Munich with FC Bayern and TSV 1860 representing differing parts of the city, differing loyalties as well as differing socio-economic groupings.

A shifting canvas

A city once could be clearly bounded – think here of city walls – with specialist zones, offices, shopping or housing, cascading out from the city core. But today city edges are permeable as they seep into the hinterland of suburbs, industrial estates and motorway junctions. The functional zone is the city region so we need to reframe what we think a city is more as a network of places with high density hubs that at times cradle clusters of activity in lower density landscapes. The polycentric place breaks the classic coherence of cities and shatters conventional views of how place and space work.

Functionally cities operate on a wider spatial canvas with transaction and trade, culture and social life at their heart. To manage consistency and efficiency in logistics or transport that cross boundaries, a bigger frame is essential. Yet city decision makers experience contradictory demands. They navigate the very local push and pull of clearing rubbish, reducing noise, curtailing crime, dealing with planning applications, making movement easy, bringing housing and health facilities up to speed, while leaving something in the kitty for culture. In sum ensuring urban services work.

City edges are permeable extending their tentacles into the surrounding hinterland.

Antwerp Behind the historic heart, a new city is emerging.

To survive well, bigger cities must play on varied stages – from the immediately local, through the regional and national, to the widest global platform. These mixed targets, goals and audiences each demand something different. Often they pull and stretch in diverging directions and can clash. One demands a local bus stop shelter, the other, airport connectivity across the world; one wants to encourage local business incubators, the other, a global brand. Working on different scales and complexity is hard: The challenge is to coalesce, align and unify this diversity so the resulting city feels coherent and can operate competently.

Cities need to speak to much wider audiences well beyond national government to attract investment, developers and the skilled and ambitious. City makers recognize they need to lure people by bonding them to place. This powerful driver that gets individuals to commit has many reasons, from being born there, to special experiences or opportunities offered. The nature of the experiences shapes the meanings that create a sense of belonging and identity.

Being small has advantages, transacting is easier, but being parochial is the danger.

A pocket sized metropolis

Small is a relative term and you do not have to be big to be successful. In a mega cities context, Barcelona or Copenhagen are small even though they operate as metropolitan entities, Catalunya or Øresund. Umea in Sweden is tiny, or in relation to power St. Etienne or Reggio Emilia are small. But as Tampere say "we are big enough, an ideal size to transact, it is easy to network." Certain conditions make being small better and you can do well being small. "We had no choice but to collaborate – it is our only asset", "in the past we could be self-sufficient" said Groningen, whose creative eco-system, straddling their university and small and large businesses was rewarded by being voted runner up in the first European Capital of Innovations awards. Or Ghent: "When you are small you have to collaborate, because you have no critical mass" and Tallinn "connecting makes you seem bigger than you are" or "you can operate on a wider scale" said Nantes.

Make the most of being small is the clarion call. At their best and when there is openness and connectivity there are competitive advantages of being smaller. Here the magic formula can work: "Small enough to make it happen, big enough to be taken seriously".

Small & ambitious

Being very small does not mean ambition fades. Ostersund in mid-Sweden saw a strategic opportunity to bid to become a Unesco Creative City of Gastronomy (2010) as a means of kickstarting regional development on a new path, but building on traditions of strong food crafts and good ingredients. It is famous for its cured meats of moose and reindeer, char, cheese, bread and chocolates. A declining population and decreasing economic prospects needed to be averted. The collaborative initiative between local food ambassador and entrepreneur Fia Gullickson and the Jamtland region's Dag Hartmann hit a nerve. It created a platform to brand the city and region by an integrated approach to growth combining the celebration of organically and sustainably produced artisan food, the healthy living agenda, promoting the slow food message, enhancing and profiling the restaurant and hospitality assets, fostering food related start-ups and so increasing employment and tourism. The strategy offers strong support to gastronomic entrepreneurs and farmers through guidance, training, product development and teaching culinary traditions. Its energetic approach has enabled Ostersund to host the Unesco network summit in 2016 which it is using as a catalyst to re-position itself at the forefront of new thinking about quality of life[1].

[1]http://unesco.seouldesign.or.kr/wp-content/uploads/2012/09/ostersundgastronomy.pdf

Size helps efficiency, where you can have six meetings in a day and everything is nearby so it is straight-forward to transact, easy to bring key parties together and so create alignment across agendas and find the agility to respond to opportunities. Comments here include from Tallinn "... it is a bit like having third space conditions, things are familiar and you know how things work ..." and from Huddersfield, "... you can get closer to citizens, our 'it's time to talk' programme worked better to explain why we as the City Council had to innovate".

The double-edged sword is the balance between being closed or open. The flipside is that smaller places are often parochial, you have less anonymity, you may not see the bigger picture, they have less resources, less connections, less credibility, less ambitious people, less power, less critical mass. But remember being too big can hamper too. Places become too complex, the play of power too convoluted, things can become dysfunctional, there is too much of everything.

Admirable smaller places can make a mark, have global resonance and overcome intrinsic disadvantages. They have some common features. They are confident, not overwhelmed by being small, are convinced that size or location does not matter and **look for strengths in each size or location**. This often means turning apparent weakness into strength.

Connections and partnerships allow them to operate on a wider scale and appear more powerful internally and externally.

'The Groningen Agreement is an alliance between the municipality and all its foreign focused universities with, among other things, its healthy ageing project. Other examples include Dublin's digital scorecard to monitor progress in the use of smart technologies or Ostersund's campaign and ambassadorial role for organic food. Strong niches help as in Freiburg[9], an old university town with 230,000 people. It is perhaps Europe's greenest city, whose long-term agenda has transformed the city physically, culturally and economically with an aim of moving towards carbon neutrality. Here there nearly as many passive houses as in entire countries, there are research centre clusters like the Fraunhofer Institute for Solar Energy, the largest in Europe with a staff of 1,300, and the European

Co-creation & everyday creativity

Umea in Sweden became the first Arctic European City of Culture in 2014 and its central theme originating in 2007 was to harness potential through 'co-creation'. This helped Umea win the award. Seen as a catalyst to unleash potential where initiatives, opportunities and problems are collaboratively conceived, executed or dealt with even if intractable, Umea aimed to change the connection between producers, audiences or users and to generate new forms of expression through two-way communication based on trust. The goal was to lead to a virtuous cycle of inventiveness and ultimately mass everyday creativity in the population. In the arts there is a history of co-creation, for instance, in improvisational theatre. Co-creation also lies at the heart of the open source software movement, where users have full access to the source code.

Examples Umea pulled off include "The Blogg-Opera" where 400 young students in vocational programmes jointly composed the libretto and music for a new opera through an innovative blogging process. Premiered in 2007 it was repeated in a collaborative co-creation venture with the opera of Hanoi. The "My Library" partnership between six municipalities to develop edge cutting library technology jointly with users was awarded the United Nations Public Sector award. "The Poet and the Prophetess" opera had its libretto and music composed collaboratively between NorrlandsOperan in Umea and Cape Town Opera and played in both cities in 2007. "The most important opera performance in Sweden for the last 15 years", reviewers said. The Research Dialogue is between children in kindergartens and professors of the University of Umea, where professors tell children about their work and research. Children paint their associations and tell professors what they believe the professors should focus on in their research. The City Council's partnership with the Institute of Design to re-design civil service operations followed the co-creation ethos

Umea wants to be first city in the world to consciously take this line forward as the next step in participatory democracy. The big question is can the momentum that launched this co-creation idea be maintained city-wide when the target of a European designation in 2014 has finished. Will the municipality understand that this is more than a cultural project[1].

[1]http://umea2014.se/en/get-involved/

Grenoble: A high tech hub part of a wider agglomeration in effect led by Lyons.

headquarters of ICLEI (International Council for Local Environmental Initiatives). In their specialist sector they have critical mass, have gathered resources, have world experts working for them, and have credibility. On a different scale Bristol's invention of the 'legible city' idea, to help people seamlessly navigate it, is now copied elsewhere. Mannheim's integrated approach to become a creative music hotspot has led to its designation as a Unesco City of Music. Meanwhile the Reggio Emilia approach in education has led to a global reputation with downstream economic impacts. The philosophy developed by Loris Malaguzzi in the early 1970s and focused on pre-school and primary education is extremely far-sighted. It goes with the grain of new trends in learning. It challenges young people to form their own personality through exploration and discovery in a supportive and enriching environment based on their interests through a self-guided curriculum.

To make their mark and be relevant to a region or country the main pre-condition for smaller places is to have strong research and learning institutions. This is why Oxford, Cambridge, Heidelberg and Padua (the highest ranked Italian university) do well economically and culturally. The shift in education thinking towards fostering knowledge transfers has spun-off into a start-up culture similar to that which originally launched Silicon Valley. Learning aside, a reputation of being creative or inventive is key, which is why Umea, in spite of being near the Arctic but with a long tradition of creativity research has flourished to become a Nordic hub. Or Huddersfield, one of the first places to involve itself in the 'creative cities' agenda in the late 1990s, has, after ups and downs, maintained its innovative DNA to recently become runner up in the Bloomberg Philanthropies innovation award for its imaginative sharing economy based Comoodle project, where 'stuff, space and skills' are shared to unleash hidden resource and under-used resources (www.comoodle.com/).

INDEPENDENCE

PEOPLES' REPUBLIC OF STOKES CROFT

WE MAKE OUR OWN FUTURE

WWW.PRSC.ORG.UK

SELL A FEW PUPPETS UNTIL I SHIFTED OFF MY MORTAL COIL. WE OWNED A PIECE OF WASTELAND

NEXT TO THE STUDIOS AND I DECIDED TO PAINT THE HOARDING FOR CHRISTMAS 2000. I HAD SEEN THE DARK WORK OF THE COUNCIL'S ANTI GRAFFITI TEAM AS THEY BUFFED OUT WITH UGLY GREY RECTANGLES THE SPARKS OF CREATIVITY THAT STOKES CROFT'S GRAFFITI COMMUNITY HAD PAINTED BY RIGHT.

AS I PAINTED PEOPLE KEPT COMING UP TO ME AND ASKING WHETHER I HAD PERMISSION TO PAINT THE FENCE. WHETHER THE COUNCIL ALLOWED ME TO PAINT IT. I WOULD POINT OUT THAT IT WAS OUR FENCE AND WE COULD DO AS WE PLEASED WITH IT. IT BECAME APPARENT THAT OUR LOCAL GOVERNMENT WAS PERCEIVED AS AN ORGANISATION WHOSE ROLE WAS TO STOP PEOPLE DOING THINGS RATHER THAN THAT OF

PUBLIC SERVANT. AS WE PAINTED WE JOKED ABOUT THE NEED TO START A REPUBLIC IN THE STYLE OF THE 1949 EALING COMEDY CLASSIC 'PASSPORT TO PIMLICO'.

IN THAT MOMENT THE PRSC WAS BORN.

CHRIS CHALKEY 2010

GRAFFITI

CINEMA

CUBE   CUBE

CHILDREN

STOKES CROFT

RUBBISH

CLOTHES

NEW TIMES & PERSPECTIVES

Elastic planning

The basic needs of cities of ambition can be summarized as follows. Make the infrastructure fit for purpose, but do so bearing in mind the urban attractors including: the look and design of the city, the attractiveness of its buildings, streetscapes and cityscape; a clean, well maintained and unpolluted place; a wide range of recreational outdoor environments, such as parks and playgrounds, cycle paths and access to nature; a rich cultural environment with many entertainment options from cafes, restaurants, markets, theatres, nightspots and sporting events; good public transport, road networks and minimal traffic congestion; a safe place; a focus on environmental sustainability; good facilities from healthcare, to schools and higher education; quality affordable housing and a good balance of different housing choices at different price ranges; employment and economic opportunities. In sum an affordable place with a good quality of life.

... the more successful you become the less affordable you are.

Here we encounter the central dilemma of city development **as the more successful you become the less affordable you are.** London, New York or San Francisco keep attracting people despite the expense, but they begin to exclude those without resources who may help the city. Provided transport connections are good this is why Bristol becomes an option for Londoners so increasing its vitality or Mannheim for Frankfurters or Rotterdam for Amsterdammers. In essence they are saying "you can make it here and we will help you". The free market on its own cannot solve this dilemma. Innovative incentives which bend the market to larger scale purposes is the way forward from discounting, to co-operative ownership or allocating a social housing proportion in exchange for planning permission. Clearly it is more difficult to do in successful places.

The world of cities is changing and with it how we plan for them. The planning and infrastructures for an industrial city are different from those where knowledge intensity is key and where individuals or organizations are encouraged to be imaginative

Bristol, a stylish university city with an alternative underbelly.

Spaces into places

There is a strategic choice between creating just one icon or doing 100 smaller things well. Icon-mania has taken hold world-wide. It continues unabated as cities try to find the physical version of the killer app that takes the world by storm and puts a city on a fast route to fame. This happens extremely rarely. The Guggenheim in Bilbao is the most notable. Yet most forget that the museum was part of an integrated, careful long term process of place management combining high quality road building, public domain work, entrepreneurship programmes and more. A roving band of nomadic starchitects, nevertheless, step over themselves to produce the most spectacular forms, proliferating gleaming glass towers, bold shapes breaking out of traditional square box patterns; skyscrapers exploding onto the landscape, some with good public spaces. Vast retailing, entertainment or cultural centres try to bewitch, enchant and seduce you.

These are supposedly the manifestations of ambition, yet reflecting ambition is more complex. Consider Malaga or Bordeaux where instead of one 'global' icon a hundred well-blended and co-ordinated initiatives are more effective than the one-off building. Malaga, once seen as the cheap holiday report for the British has brought its extensive old city to life by expensively under-grounding all car parking, upgrading housing, and bringing out its Andalusian qualities in innovative schemes like canvas sun shading of streets. Yes - it also has a major strategy to connect to global museums like the State Russian Museum in St. Petersburg and a Pop Up Pompidou.

Bordeaux has been able to overcome the people and place conundrum by an ambitious regeneration programme launched in the mid-1990s by the mayor Alain Juppe (later France's prime minister). Once many avoided the city, apart from the wine business. It had many classical buildings in the largely 18th-century urban core that were grimy and the streets dirty and clogged with traffic and ugly warehouses cut the city off from the river. The cleaned up limestone facades changed perceptions and the popular waterfront promenade packed with strollers, joggers and skateboarders. By seamlessly connecting tram and bus modes across the centre and suburbs as well as electric bus shuttles the city has been given back to people with many pedestrianised streets and squares along their routes. The Chartrons neighbourhood where its bric-abrac shops were based is now like the Marais in Paris. The youthful feel is enhanced by the Darwin Ecosysteme, a 3-hectare 'eco-creative business incubator' where nearly 500 people work in over 120 SMEs and associations. A 'fluid place', they say "where different cultural and economic dynamics come together to create a genuine ecosystem for creativity and frugality". And crucially housing is not forgotten. The Bassin-a-flots scheme will create a new urban district for 10,000 residents.

and to feel commitment to your place. In the one, people are seen simply as units of mechanical production while, in the other, as the key ideas (and thus wealth) generators. This is recasting the planning paradigm. The physical infrastructure and design differ, as public space – or providing the context for people to meet – and good sensory environments are crucial. Walkability, good connectivity, convenient public transport and many third spaces are needed.

A crisp encapsulation: Here in Torino graffiti tells the story of a central urban dilemma.

Planning needs an elastic framework to reflect emerging needs. Malmo calls this **non-linear planning**. Planning for places that encourage people to feel anchored yet creative has a different operating dynamic, logic and priorities from traditional spatial planning. It is more concerned with creating environments for exchange and knowledge sharing that are satisfactory from a sensory perspective. Yet in any planning for cities some basic issues remain consistent. Clearly traditional planning, with its focus on land uses, how space is organized or where differing types of settlement should occur, continues as do planning decisions about infrastructures such as roads, utilities like electricity or sewage. But the roads and the utilities will feel different as planners focus both on the software as well as the hardware of the city. The hardware focus has shaped the discipline of planning and the skills applied. These were based largely on engineering, architecture and surveying. These groups have a certain mindset that is both positive and negative. The culture of engineering is logical, rational and technologically adept, but often has less sensitivity about how places feel. The new planner understands the emotional and psychological life of cities.

Obstacles and dilemmas

The major frustrations and obstacles affecting cities across Europe fall into four principal categories: objective conditions – such as poverty, the brain drain, old infrastructure, or ambition thwarted by lack of finance; second, control over resources and lack of power; third, mindset, 'the culture' and the 'system'; and lastly, political power play and associated human frailties.

Patience & ambition

The Ruhr area and Emscher Park within is Germany's most industrialized zone and was home to Krupp and Thyssen. Incorporating partners across a region its regeneration is one of the most comprehensively considered and innovatively conceived and implemented. A dense urban agglomeration of 5.3 million people and one of Europe's most heavily urbanized and industrialized areas, its principal cities include Essen, Dortmund, Bochum, Gelsenkirchen and Duisburg. By 1987 a major crisis of deep structural significance unfolded, whose cataclysmic proportions stretched far beyond the factory gate. The environmental legacy left scars on the landscape and extreme degradation. Starting with an emblematic 30 year vision and clarion call to 'renature' the Emscher river 'Von Kloake zum Fluss' - from sewer to clean river. Solving a problem of epic proportions was aimed at changing the ecology, economy, culture and social life. Steeped in the semi-feudal mentality of the old corporatism the dominance of large corporations had debilitating effects on entrepreneurialism. Degradation was used as an opportunity to create new products and services with stringent standard setting and legislation helping to drive the innovative process. The result 25 years later is 150 R&D centres; technology transfer offices; technology centres and agencies to nurture new businesses and innovations. Many of the factories, 'cathedrals in the desert', played their part in helping a 'culture change without erasing memory'. The approach was called 'incrementalism with perspective'. Especially powerful is the conversion of Europe's largest gasholder in Oberhausen into an exhibition centre. This landmark spurred the development of Germany's largest shopping centre CentrO next door. Second was changing Europe's vast coal mine Zeche Zollverein into conference facilities, museums, leisure and an industrial design centre. The latter, adapted by Norman Foster, left the grime and tools of the past as they lay on closure. The third was transforming the stunning structures of the steel works in Duisburg-Meiderich into a landscape park: Duisburg Nord. The factory becomes a nightly spectacular as visitors clamber up the steel structures in the dark designed by Jonathan Park of Pink Floyd fame.

Managed by the IBA (Internationale Bauaustellung) from 1989 to 1999 its powers were indirect levers, its political status and the IBA label on projects which gave prestige and its role was to act as a gateway to help bundle resources. Once finished the focus of the area subsequently shifted to creating a 'route of industrial culture' as well a strategy to establish creative quarters based on creative industry activities such as gaming Without the IBA to drive things the momentum has of course decreased.

http://www.gamesfactory-ruhr.de/

Malaga: The public space strategy of the city is increasingly admired.

All places in transition have been affected by the global financial crisis since 2008 and this has exacerbated existing attempts to transform themselves into more knowledge-driven economies with appropriate activity and animation programmes or physical infrastructures to match. Even though endemic skill problems and entrenched poverty remain they are all in a better condition being active rather than passive. Many of the external conditions are outside of their control.

Yet how bureaucracies are run or organizational culture and even mindset can be changed. When assets are scarce, being well-run and providing good orchestration are among the few resources a city has left. **"Good organization is our new competitive tool"**. Quotes from across Europe such as Barcelona explain things well: "my main lesson of 30 years' experience in the public and private world is if you do not manage to break siloes you cannot do real business".

Cities of Ambition

*Dortmund in the Ruhr area - a vast
long term regeneration initiative
recognized across the globe.*

A different bureaucracy

Pressures for municipalities to think afresh about their role, how they perform and how they relate to their communities are increasing. Reduced funds, at times by 40%, has forced the pace and created the trigger to act. Many have slimmed down, used IT to save costs and cut budgets. But to keep up services and outcomes with drastically less resources demands different ways of operating.

Kirklees and its New Council, where Huddersfield is based, stands as an example for many to reinvent the bureaucracy. The words used in their new corporate plan 2015-16 are revealing and their 1 million euros prize winning Bloomberg innovation scheme Comoodle shows their thinking in action. Here is a flavour:

"Our mission is to be a modern, flexible and emotionally intelligent organisation and to become a radically ambitious enabling council that connects ideas, people and resources across boundaries of all kinds... a council focused on creating trust and synergy between the institutions, businesses and citizens in Kirklees. Our cross party principles involve all five political parties - the Labour Party, the Conservative Party, the Liberal Democrat Party, the Green Party and the Valley Independent Party. We agree to 12 cross party principles to lead the Council's approach. We believe that the transformation to a New Council necessitates clear agreement between them... We will be mindful of the market and the local mixed economy and we will establish partnerships with appropriate private companies and community organisations to maximise income from the Council estate... Devolution should be, as far as possible, to communities... People are more important than buildings... We will create conditions where business and wealth grow naturally and is retained in the district.

"A consistent level of basic services will be available to residents across the district, but at a lower level than now... The role of the councillor is refocused as community leader, building community capacity in their wards and actively encouraging people to do more for themselves and each other... The way we work together between councillors and officers will have to change, as will the expectations we have of each other.

"The Council has five 'Wildly Important Goals' for all of our staff... We expect all our staff to be able to honestly say:

• I know exactly the difference my work makes for local people.

• I spend every Council pound as if it were my own, including my time and other peoples' time.

• I work with whoever I need to, across the Council and outside of it, to make a real difference.

• I am creative and I empower people to do more things for themselves and each other.

• I'm a 'can do' person - I don't avoid challenges or taking risks.

In 2014, a series of events across Kirklees called 'It's time to talk' talked about budget reductions with locals and community organisations about doing things differently and how people could get involved.

"To deliver this vision and respond to budget challenges, we recognise that the New Council must work in a different and more ambitious way. All leaders in Kirklees agree that transforming from the old Council to New Council will require: a new relationship with our communities and citizens, with local people doing more for themselves and each other, a continued focus on using scarce resources well,... greater collaboration with our public sector partners, businesses and community organisations to connect ideas, people and resources. As far as possible, the Council wants to support peopleto help themselves... we want to be truly enabling."

The Comoodle project exemplified this (http://www.comoodle.com/about-us/)

The head of strategy John Heneghan said: "It's a really exciting time for collaboration. Companies such as Netflix, Uber, Airbnb and Zipcar are rewriting the rule book on how we access and share resources. The time has come to redesign how we manage public resources. We have lots of underused resources in the local authority, vans, buildings that were underused and we had skills in the council and wondered how you could make more use of it. We found a partner in Collaborative Lab in San Francisco and they helped our expression of interest for Bloomberg. The idea fitted our vision is centred around making the most of skills, resources and assets that exist on 'The Street' in Kirklees. So Comoodle sought to mobilise the energy, talents and passion of people in Kirklees."

Beguiling the government

Late, perhaps too late, Britain realized that cities need self-determination. Centralized Britain "is having a centrifugal moment" and as the prime minister said after the Scottish independence elections shook Britain to its bones "it is time to empower our great cities". Manchester has been chosen to lead the revival as the engine of a Northern powerhouse connecting 10 million people across a wider metropolis. Whitehall, the central civil service, unwilling to cede power, was side-lined in the negotiations as several hundred million pounds were devolved.

The situation is urgent with the British North/South divide exacerbating and long term promises to rebalance having had little effect. Between 2004 -2013 for every job created in the North there were 12 in the South.

Manchester's political acumen, its consistency, reliability and ability to deliver what government wants made it the obvious choice. Its forward-thinking long-term planning, with a political leader and CEO in joint harness for two decades, has attracted foreign investment and built trust that they will deliver. Manchester has been able to implement national experiments, such as creating with the 10 metro boroughs Greater Manchester Combined Authority with its own mayor. They have received special concessions such as receiving £78million for a new theatre called the Factory whilst others cities, like Bristol and Birmingham, have had to dramatically cut cultural budgets and are irritated by this special treatment for Manchester[1].

[1]http://www.ft.com/cms/s/2/a0513f2a-b7bb-11e4-981d-00144feab7de.html#slide0

Bureaucratic inventiveness

... bureaucracies in the public, private and community sectors need to change dramatically.

Ambition can be thwarted by old-fashioned organizations and leadership models. Thus many cities have explored how to rethink their bureaucracy including Ghent with its horizontal working strategies that has created great loyalty from its staff[10] or Mannheim with its CHANGE[2] process[11] or Kirklees with its New Council reorganization[12]. A global movement is emerging to focus on developing creative bureaucracies[13]. Practically all successful cities have made concerted efforts to use IT systems to streamline services especially using 'big data' techniques. This focus on efficiency is necessary, but does not necessarily change the culture. Ghent notes: "too much emphasis is on effectiveness and accountancy-driven thinking which leads to cold organizations. This lack of organizational emotion cannot inspire staff. The atmosphere needs to be 'warm' to develop an R&D culture.

The intense frustration experienced by some of the best minds in public service cannot be over-stated. The refrain, constantly repeated is the problem of the silo, a lack of integrated and holistic thinking, the inability to cross boundaries, the reluctance to see the benefits of interdisciplinary working or unwillingness to truly partner across divisions or to connect imaginatively with outside worlds. People say "the inertia is immense' and "inflexibility does not allow you respond effectively". "I wanted a 'yes', but it is so much easier to say 'no'". "With silo thinking the ability to work across departments or sectors never develops" and "thus no skill in partnering evolves". It leads to "the tendency to look inwards rather than outwards" and this "the cost of narrow minded thinking is difficult to calculate". "All I know is that some of the best people are leaving", and "we find it hard to hold on to the young and enthusiastic, they start with energy and then feel drained as they bump into barriers".

Crucially "it is difficult to appoint the best or get the worst to leave, trade unions are strong although important to have, but they need to adapt and learn that this is about serving the public" and "the environment of risk aversion that does not understand the difference between risk and uncertainty". "Doing nothing can seem safe, as then nobody is to blame" and "the biggest risk is taking no risks", "reinforced when politicians know that population itself is too critical of the bold".

Add to this brew the human frailties of power play, factionalism, micro-politics, jealousy or blatant resistance. Is the individual, the organization or the system at fault?[14] The response mostly is to re-organize structures, to deal with staff or efficiency problems. Yet "organizational change is easy, culture change difficult" and a debilitating reform fatigue is noticeable. Overall this reduces the discretionary effort people put in when conditions are good. Our separate survey on bureaucratic creativity estimates that people operate under par and could put on average 35% more effort in if the "system had less out of date rules and entrenched attitudes or old fashioned leadership thinking".

City & state

The relationship between city and state strongly determines how ambitious cities can be. Many conclude that their prospects are constrained by lack of money raising capacities and power especially in Europe and most of Asia. This plays itself out differently in various countries with Germany or Spain delegating more and both Britain and France being among the most centralized countries in Western Europe. Until recently Britain's strongest political parties have infantilized British cities, controlling the purse strings with a gut reaction that claims the centre knows best. This London-centric approach intensely irritates the other cities. The barriers "do not allow us to compete effectively" and creates a dependency culture in which there is less urban innovation than there should be. The "government punishes failure too much and rewards success too little", "it

Eindhoven: Woensel West an exceptional area transformation - see the Game Changer box overleaf.

does not know how to make us enthusiastic" and given how far away it is from problems on the ground "is not good at assessing new more exploratory initiatives, with the Treasury using old-fashioned narrowly focused cost-benefit approaches to assess things". There is insufficient understanding of the value of intangibles and this constrains daring. Contrast this with the progressive Spanish cities – such as Bilbao, Barcelona, Valencia and Malaga – or the former German industrial areas like Essen, Dortmund and Leipzig where self-determination as well as central government help drives motivation and will. At last the British government in 2015 has realized that it must loosen power as it cannot achieve its objectives of job creation, inward investment and competitiveness from the centre. Here Manchester has become the poster child at the centre of the new Northern engine in an attempt to rebalance the British economy – and Manchester has responded with imagination. Similar top down approaches are seen in France.

Skills imbalance

Public administrations have been decried as inefficient, driven by red tape and lacking skills. Some criticism is valid but it is not the norm or intention. This demotivates and makes public service less likely to be a career choice with the private sector picking up the best people. It is exacerbated by negative media who rarely acknowledge good· work or a positive role for public interest organizations whose purpose is to help deliver services with balance, fairness and transparency. At the same time cities of all sizes recognize how public finance problems have exacerbated since the 2008 financial crisis.

All governments face a convoluted and exacerbating situation of decreasing incomes and increasing demands on expenditure. Income from taxation has declined with less economic activity and with greater unemployment the personal tax take has reduced.

Additional trends make the need for new thinking inevitable, especially thinking about partnering that require refined skills to make it happen. They include the 'cost disease' and inexorable growth in demand and expectations for more public services and more quality that have risen over the last 60 years as has the scope of services. The desire for services like health, social welfare, education or leisure provision can be nearly limitless and at the same time new needs evolve such as demands to help entrepreneurialism, business incubation and economic development in general.

The 'cost disease' is the tendency for the cost of personal services to rise persistently and cumulatively faster than the rate of inflation as cumulative data from well over 100 years shows. This notably affects healthcare, education, legal services and live artistic performances and associated facilities which are difficult to make more productive through technology. This has led the public sector to seek partnerships with private and community based organizations.

These partnerships are often sophisticated and require highly skilled people to negotiate them. But **too often the skills have gone in the public sector.**

The connector

The role of the connector is vital for cities to fulfil their ambitions. It is undervalued and even unseen. At their best these are people who have an overview of what is happening in a given area and how to make the most of potential by bringing people, networks or organizations together. They try to stand above the fray and focus on what really matters by bringing ideas and opportunity together. They take an eagle eye on things and rove over concerns. They look for the common agenda. They can see issues that many organizations view as quite important, but not as of prime importance - often because it is not their main raison d'etre. As most organizations work in silos, crucial issues can slip through under-acknowledged, yet they may be the most important task for a city. These could be: the level of confidence in a city; opportunities arising from unusual partnerships such as mixing older and younger generations or science, technology and the arts worlds; or bringing together social entrepreneurs with more traditional business people where others would not see the connection.

The connector has a difficult role to play. They need to present themselves as beyond self-interest and have authority but not exert power explicitly. They need influence to draw credible people and organizations together, and often they need to shape the agenda. If they take too much credit others will be jealous, yet at the same they need some authority or accrued credit to change the way people operate. The connector needs an unusual set of qualities, including a sharp focus, clarity, strategic intent, diplomatic skills, flexibility, the capacity to read situations and deal with power play, strong conceptual thinking to understand the essence of arguments, summarizing skills, and the ability to chair and make meetings work.

Aligning time frames

The complex activities of city making happen in differing time frames. This **makes orchestration a crucial task and significant new skill**. Some are immediate and urgent such as emergency services, others stretch into the far horizon and up to 20 years with shorter and medium term plans in between. The pace of business and strategic urban planning often do not align, but the population needs to feel things are on the move. Substantive interventions to refit urban infrastructure take a very long time – 30 year projects such as rejuvenating the Emscher river or creating the new Spina 2,3,4 in Torino or 22@ Barcelona. The new Kalasatamaa district in Helsinki, Kop van Zuid or new station area in Rotterdam or renewing Isle de Nantes will take 20 years.

Creating commitment to a proposed physical vision is vital as is maintaining momentum when projects begin to get underway. The achievable goal needs to remain in view and this is where artistry, imagery and programming can help and, most importantly, delivering early wins. The storytelling used, for instance, by Antwerp (see separate box) has been important in giving confidence to the vast spatial redevelopments underway, which by definition are contentious. Prefiguring the future becomes key as does providing a step-by-step sense of forward movement. Here orchestrating the easy, cheap and short-term achievable to give confidence for the difficult, more expensive and longer-term is significant. Many cities use cultural events linked to wider strategies for city development. Three examples suffice.

The living artwork *"Still life:Ruhrschnellweg"* or the "Ruhr Speedway", part of Ruhr 2010 when it was European City of Culture, ensured there were "bars not cars, culture not cargo" as one of the Germany's busiest highways, the A40, closed for a day along a stretch of 60 kms between Duisburg and Dortmund. Two million people celebrated along the world's longest table made up of 20,000 parts along the north side. There were cultural activities and also school reunions, birthday parties and even weddings. The south side was filled with cyclists, skateboarders and walkers. The message was about identifying the Ruhr as a cohesive metropolis and recapturing the public realm by showing the experience of car-free environments[15].

St. Etienne's Cite du Design and its *Biennale* combines the regeneration of a giant old munitions factory, one of the France's largest, into an international exhibition centre, the site of its art and design school, with an incubator centre called *Mixeur*. The *Biennale* thematically focused and assertive is different from a trade show. Its focus has included

A game changer

In the 1970s, Woensel West, a once homogenous working class neighbourhood, became mixed and diverse as low skilled workers first from South Europe and then Turkey and Morocco fed the assembly lines of Philips and DAF. The neighbourhood changed dramatically, it became less cohesive and social conflicts rose. The more ambitious Dutch left and tenants with little perspective stayed and so began its decline exacerbated by the rise of organised crime as women, often trafficked, from Eastern Europe and Africa provided sex services that were once offered by local tenants. Woensel-West slowly grew as the main meeting point for all kinds of criminals and especially drug dealers. Security was the main problem not only for women but also children. Needles and condoms were everywhere.

The neighbourhood then received special 'urban renewal status' whose goal was to end 'deprivation' with extra budgets to renovate houses, improve public space and to organize social activities. It failed partly because of the economic recession and especially the decline of Philips, secondly many people leaving psychiatric institutions were housed in the district.

The housing association Trudo took over this complex problem and became convinced traditional policies would not work. They needed a dramatic game changer. It started with security, the greatest concern. They focused on prostitution and, in collaboration with the police, managed everything very strictly. After more than three years with constant threats to Trudo, finally prostitution was severely contained and women could walk in the evening and children could play in the public space.

But what to do next given the high rate of unemployment, the physical condition of houses, the language deficiency, the lack of social cohesion, the quality of public space, the bad results of the primary school, health care problems and so on. The instinctive reaction is to deal with the physical, but central to the new vision was transforming Woensel-West into an attractive place for young people and to end the concentration of poor and under-privileged people,

The vision had three pillars: emancipate the kids, then think of the physical and lastly build a reputation for the area that helps people get jobs. For target one, instead of just bringing in teachers they brought in younger people. They asked for volunteers who would get a discounted rental house in exchange for investing 10 hours every month in supporting the kids.

Despite cynicism and fierce opposition, the results were amazing. Now 180 young people, give 1800 hours every month supporting 350 kids in learning Dutch, doing homework, helping the transition from primary to secondary schools or organizing activities.

The main result is that the kids are no longer a lost generation. They are curious, eager to learn, proud. And the big surprise. The Woensel-West kids received the best education score for South Netherlands, well above the average. A (potential) lost generation is an ambitious generation and their video: 'we are the smartest children' engenders self-confidence. These results have had downstream effects on the attitude of the parents[1].

[1] http://www.trudo.nl/ and http://www.strijp-s.nl/nl/home

A creative ecology

Groningen, the regional power of northern Netherlands, once semi-independent and member of the German Hanseatic League, has a collaborative ethos: "We have no choice but to collaborate – it is our only asset and chance". The willingness to collaborate requires "not much social hierarchy" and "we have to be open-minded". Once it was Groningen's self-containment and isolation that was an asset that etched itself into the DNA, "but in the contemporary world that is not enough, now networks and connectivity are key". "We are always looking for horizontal connections with universities, citizen and business". "We have no big company, not a lot of money, lots of clever young people so we make ourselves bigger by collaborating". "We need open officials, we call ourselves entrepreneurial civil servants or the civil servant 2.0". "We do not want to be a referee like in football, we want to go beyond being the conductor or facilitator , that is old-fashioned, we want to be an equal player." "I am surprised the private companies don't get this."

Groningen had rigid leaders until the 1970s then there was a power takeover by the 1960s generation and in 1972 the average age of councillors dropped to 24 years. This "stopped the old way of thinking, stopped moving a hospital to outskirts, or a motorway going through the city". They allowed new experimental mental space to develop.

This has allowed an integrated innovation system to develop with the University at its heart. A global hub of connections, it has created the global fluency required to make the creative ecology work. This is anchored in a strategic alliance called 'The Groningen Agreement 2.0: Investing Together in Knowledge & Innovation.' Its healthy ageing centre is a network organization. Its inventive 'smart energy citizen' initiative has become a living lab where 1000s of households take part. Groningen's Smart Energy City (GROSEC) is challenging and disruptive as it shifts the balance of power from energy markets and large energy providers to citizens. They help develop new concepts and apps in a co-creative way with R&D partners and with interesting projects like Smart Energy Battles are attracting talents from elsewhere.

These successes encouraged Groningen to bid for the European Capital of Innovation 2014 award, where it was runner up with Grenoble to Barcelona. That has triggered further ambition and new connections with Barcelona a city 10 times its size[1].

[1]http://ec.europa.eu/research/innovation-union/indexen.cfm?section=icapital

Torino: Courageous building by Luciano Pia in an old FIAT property that is revitalizing the area.

human cities, teleportation, and a sense of beauty. It seeks to remind the city of its immense design tradition and adapt these to the new era as well as to embed design thinking into city development and acts as a catalyst for innovation and company growth[16].

Torino is a capital of the Slow Food movement whose headquarters are in nearby Bra 60 kms away. It has become a global movement to shift how we think of food production, local entrepreneurship and quality of living. Torino wants to be identified as a hub for this new thinking and is gearing many programmes towards this aim, such as in food-related design at its Applied Arts and Design University as well as hosting the major Slow Food event *Salone del Gusto* and *Tierra Madre*[17] at the famous former FIAT factory Lingotto, so signalling a symbolic change in focus.

... to create the change in mindset often requires a shift in personnel.

THE QUALITIES OF AMBITION

The lessons cities with ambition offer to others are varied, but most **importantly there is a narrative drive** and a story that feels compelling and gives everyone a role in its unfolding.

Character & essence

The vision of place links to the past and acknowledges its virtues, but moves on in drawing out a picture of what can be and how you can get there. It is achievable, yet with a touch of extra aspiration that unleashes in the community a sense of verve and 'can do'. In so doing it drives momentum. To do this they:

• Try to gain confidence from being themselves.

•Identify, harness and orchestrate collective intelligence and resources by bringing the disparate parties together who have an effect on urban change, growth and well-being.

• Integrate the differing perspectives in conceiving, planning and implementing initiatives and plans and they recognize the power of specialist knowledge, but are not beholden to it.

• Understand that value and insight comes from looking at issues in a cross-cutting way. This implies breaking out of the silo thinking and re-assessing how rules can be adapted to the issues that really matter and any resulting vision.

• Know that the new often under-valued skills are required. such as how to connect to and partner with others, and being relaxed about ambiguity.

• Catalyse change by finding big game changers, like major award schemes or on occasion a building. They also pursue the slow burners where many small projects threaded together coherently become the equivalent of something large.

There follow some qualities and characteristics of ambitious places with the briefest reminder of some cities that exemplify those attributes. Of course, nowhere is going to have all these qualities, but our ambitious cities will share a significant proportion of them.

Malmo: Western Harbour a model for carbon neutral urban development.

Courage, tenacity & boldness

• Crisis is seen as an opportunity to take responsibility, to be bold and look at things afresh.

• Ambitious places recognize that the operating dynamics of cities are changing and that new competitive resources are coming to the fore.

• They look at the bigger picture, they think forward and plan backwards. Their thinking is strategic. They assess the future in the broadest terms. They exhibit foresight and awareness beyond the confines of their own discipline, field and interests and are conscious that they are helping to future-proof their city.

• Their city leaderships, public and private, **create a crisis of ambition** - a crisis of a special kind - here aspiration pushes a city forward. With a normal crisis threats loom sharply and action is required and for the complacent problems can be addressed too late.

Bilbao was bold when it grasped the opportunity and a capacity to attract the prestigious Guggenheim museum with multiple subsequent spin-offs. Malmo had courage when it used the 1989 crisis to create a revitalized city nearly from scratch. The Emscher Park/ Ruhr area showed prolonged tenacity to refit an old industrial region into a modern knowledge-driven economy.

Progressive administration

• Good urban governance is the sine qua non of success as is using resources effectively. The administration is seen as transparent, clear and focused and well-organized. Working with others they create mature, motivated partnerships with private and third sector organizations. This increasingly becomes the norm.

• They are not only collegiate, but collaborative and so make the most of their potential.

• The rules and incentives system are adapted to the emerging vision of the city rather than existing rules constraining potential. They think through new financing mechanisms to achieve objectives.

• This enhances the ability to construct more flexible mechanisms to achieve the complex deals focused on creating public interest outcomes.

Ghent's administration has a progressive, forward focused atmosphere that makes public service a desirable career choice. Tallinn is a leader in rethinking how to communicate with citizens and to make new technology work for them. Mannheim is seeking to shift the German administrative system to one that is more flexible.

Farsighted vision

• Being farsighted and understanding global dynamics is considered a central leadership virtue to achieve ambitions. The ability to place the possibilities for the city in a broader context and see how they fit in is vital.

• Being strategically principled and tactically flexible helps frame the city's modus operandi, guided by a determined delivery focus.

• There is an ability to tell a story of place and how everyone might fit in.

• The capacity to orchestrate the short, cheaper and easier initiatives with longer term, less easy and more expensive ones is crucial is achieve momentum and to add value.

Freiburg was well ahead of the world when it used the Chernobyl crisis of 1986 as a trigger to re-shift its energy systems and is now a world leader. Lille reconfigured how it would be placed in the world through strategic moves, most notably getting the Eurostar station. Helsinki's urban research department and its associated networks think deeply and long-term to link strategic social goals to those of economic vitality.

Honest about realities

• A realistic assessment and deep understanding of economic prospects and problems shapes strategic thinking and develops urgency.

• There is an openness and transparency about overcoming obstacles.

• Programmes exist to help bring people from the old economy into the new.

St. Etienne's mayor Michel Thiollière risked deep unpopularity to launch a major renewal programme and was later voted out, only to re-emerge when the benefits became clear. Eindhoven faced its crisis head-on and dug into its industrial DNA to recast its asset base for tomorrow's world. The same is true for Torino whose escalating crisis forced a dramatic rethink.

Widespread leadership

• Departments and sectors are willing to work together and to develop a culture of collaboration. Integrated thinking, planning and acting is seen are increasingly the norm. Interdisciplinary working is encouraged. There is an understanding that not all wisdom is to be found within the public administration and so cooperation with many stakeholders is the key to success.

• There are many leaders and many levels of leadership. Leadership is seen as a discipline and resource that can be learnt and overrides power play. Possibilities exist to create widespread leadership groupings with decision making communities in public and private walks of life. These have a forward focus, whether they are teachers, public servants, transports chiefs, middle and higher management in industry and business, or community organisers or those in the artistic world.

• There are dynamic and forward looking people of quality in every sector providing a strong sense of vision for the place, with deep awareness of current and emerging trends and their implications.

• There is an infectious professional pride. The culture and leadership style is inspiring, able to delegate and be empowering to others. Things are accessible. These leaders describe an achievable yet ambitious future that acts as a compelling and involving story.

The idea of leadership and citizen involvement is progressively being rethought.

Barcelona is challenging itself to think afresh about how to lead and who leads the city, with greater citizen involvement a central goal. There is even a 'Children as Planners' project. It is by harnessing its combined technical, intellectual and political capacities that Copenhagen has made so much of its potential. Groningen has shown that the power of collaboration can make smaller cities come across as bigger.

Sophisticated learning landscapes

• The move to the knowledge intensive economy demands outward looking learning institutions adept at understanding how new learning and communications systems work.

• A culture of debate fosters an environment of openness and this is encouraged by awards, recognition schemes and the encouragement of experimental practices.

• A culture of self-development, learning and foresight is encouraged with appropriate mechanisms to match.

• Learning does not only happen in universities, but also other settings such as centres of excellence or professional development contexts.

Helsinki and Espoo's far-sighted merger of three universities – arts and design, natural science and economics – into Aalto is seen as a model for the new thinking about integrated learning. Reggio

Helsinki: The elegiac Kamppi chapel of silence – a haven in the city.

Emilia has become a global leader in new forms of teaching that start from the child outwards so affecting the learning system as a whole.

Harnessing all talents

• Cities have a talent attraction and retention strategy and nurture and mobilize the ideas, talents and creative organizations in their city in order to retain the young and gifted.

• Ladders of opportunity are created to generate good transitions between the world of learning and work. Often this involves setting up incubation and co-working networks and centres of excellence. The link between research worlds and industry is productive.

• Younger cohorts are encouraged to grow through mentoring programmes in the public and private sectors so that leadership qualities cascade down the organizational structure.

... it is increasingly important to harness the collective imagination and intelligence of cities.

Rotterdam has made itself the hub of the Dutch Creative Residency network, a grouping of 33 older buildings across the Netherlands housing 4000 start-ups. Bristol's two universities are overcoming traditional rivalries and collaborating on robotics research and establishing incubators together in order to make the most of resources. Mannheim has a well-developed formal and informal learning system that creates good ladders of opportunity.

Bi-partisanship & active citizens

• Bi-partisanship on the major issues concerning the city is seen as crucial both within the political class as well as with the private sector. This involves bringing public and private partners together on jointly agreed agendas.

• Citizens are activated on a larger scale and initiatives exist to seek their involvement as shapers, makers and co-creators.

Manchester has been at the forefront in creating strategic alliances between city and state to mutual benefit, achieving possibilities that otherwise would not be available. Bristol's new leadership is attempting to blow the dust off old party political attitudes that have been holding the city back. The Umea 2014 European City of Culture process helped unleash citizen participation on an unusual scale. The challenge is whether it can continue.

Collaborating across boundaries

• A core ethos is to create an environment that opens up opportunities and does not over contain sensible proposals and activities.

• A well-respected multi-disciplinary 'thinking brain' for the city made up of private and public sector partners is seen as essential. Part of their work is sophisticated auditing of urban assets and resources and obstacles to success. This evaluation happens on a continuing basis.

Malmo has been able to bring together public, private and community forces across the city to focus on agreed aims for city growth and its university has a strong reputation for cross-disciplinary subjects attracting widespread talents. The Groningen Agreement to maximize potential between the city and university on healthy ageing and new energy system has become a model. Within the Unesco Creative Cities music network Bologna, Mannheim and Ghent are attempting to broaden the scope, relevance and impact of music on society.

Transparent, inclusive processes

• There is a well-balanced combined top down and bottom approach that recognizes both the value of citizens and external specialists.

• The public institutions combine a listening capacity yet simultaneously are willing to be bold and have a clear standpoint when necessary.

• A default position exists to involve people and organizations even though it takes more time and with an understanding that this helps create resilience.

All 30 cities surveyed are re-focusing their decision-making procedures to make them more involving. They recognize that creating inclusive processes makes their city ultimately more prosperous, increases ownership of the outcomes of city development and thus more resilient. Tampere, Dublin and Hamburg are good places to explore.

... only by working across disciplines and sectors can cities bring out the most of possibilities.

Dublin has become even more vibrant so attracting companies in the new economy.

Hubs & hotspots

• Creating areas where critical mass can be established focused on niches like designated business or creative economy districts.

• Spreading renewal initiatives across the city to create alternative hotspots including collaborative workspaces.

• Developing a networked incubator and breeding ground strategy.

A dynamic start-up culture is emerging with many focusing on 'sharing economy' ideas.

Ostersund has become a Swedish food hotspot through a co-ordinated hospitality and food production strategy. This gives hope to the vast number of smaller places. Malaga has used being a cruise liner destination and surprised the urban community by developing a new series of museums with major global partners. Amsterdam's breeding ground strategy is the best known, but all places surveyed from Rotterdam to Bordeaux are establishing interesting start-up venues and clusters.

Balancing the big & small

• Not being too focused on creating single big icons at the expense of taking budgets from other initiatives.

• Seeking to avoid overwhelming and over-scale comprehensive development schemes.

• Creating master planning frameworks that allow for a diversity of housing choices.

• Orchestrating well thought-through smaller initiatives that in their totality are the equivalent of a large icon so celebrating the fine grain.

Bordeaux and Bristol, with its legible city strategy, as instances are focusing on the fine grain of city making. Bilbao started with an icon strategy, it has now spread out the regeneration dynamic to Zorrozaure an artificial peninsula, but whether this can attract smaller projects and companies remains to be seen. Ile de Nantes, also a peninsula, seems to have the mix right with both the big Les Machines de l'ile and also high-tech Incubators[19].

Mainstream & alternative

• Being relaxed about encouraging alternatives that challenge the status quo.

• Instituting a balanced support structure to ensure creativity is embedded in how the urban dynamic evolves.

• Celebrating imagination, creativity and imagination through innovation schemes and recognition programmes.

Berlin's counter- culture scene was part of the city's rebirth. Helsinki has developed a vibrant alternative scene exemplified by projects such as 'restaurant day' or the start-up festival *Slush* as well as classic institution-building such as its new library[18]. The alternative scene in Manchester is renowned and encouraged by public authorities such as its international festival of original new work and special events.

Diversity & openness

• Highlighting and working with the diversity advantage.

• Fostering a culture of openness and ensuring this is manifested in all areas of public life.

• Expressing diversity in the built form.

To be open is the main criterion for a successful city. Copenhagen, Zurich and Oslo have been voted the top three inclusive cities in Europe in fighting against discrimination[20].

Highlighting cultural distinctiveness

• Identifying the unique, special and distinctive and promoting this accordingly.

• Using cultural programmes as an attractor and thus helping develop a strategy of confidence.

• Using artistic interventions to generate a sense of wonder.

• Using the city as a stage and canvas to express itself.

• Orchestrating a calendar with locally derived and internationally oriented events.

A mere mention of any city surveyed and a different picture of place emerges: Freiburg, somewhat comfortable and stable looking; Bologna the university city par excellence and with the wild graffiti to match; Tampere, like many unpretentious places, a practical city that is what it is – a gritty place with an invigorating cultural programme to match.

Measuring against the best

• Good mechanisms exist to gather information on good practices and innovative solutions from around the globe, such as research centres and collaborative devices such as cluster networks, specialist hubs or centres of excellence.

• All parties are alert and scan the horizon in their respective sectors, actively looking out for the next important thing in their respective domains – currently there is likely to a significant involvement in things green. Pride in place helps the city share a common agenda.

Good examples are the Network of Urban Laboratories co-ordinated by TU-Berlin or the Grenoble and Torino cultural observatories, Helsinki city's Tietokeskus and Amsterdam's OIS office.

Strategically opportunistic

• They are strategically agile knowing when and how to seize opportunities, for which they have already created a state of preparedness.

• Creating a bidding machine constantly alert to opportunities.

• Seeing the planning process as continuous and not as a one off activity. They survey the world to pick up projects and competitions where they can test themselves and further their purposes. These are assessed in terms of the legacy they can build and how they can take the city forward.

Practically all the cities surveyed have won major competitive awards including the European Green City, European City of Culture or City of Innovation, the Bloomberg Challenge or the UN Public Sector Award. In scanning the horizon they avoided a scatter-

Awards & competitions

Competing for awards and challenges are one of the best ways for cities to focus on who they are, what assets they have and what they want to be. In addition the aim is to grab attention, gain respect, change perceptions, highlight certain sectors, initiate catalytic processes and to get onto the radar screen. Crucially there is a time-dated target that often encourages things to be done in innovative ways as well as fostering organizations to work collaboratively.

The larger awards for hosting the football world cup or Olympics are out of reach for most, yet were once most crucial in retrofitting physical infrastructure and building new facilities as happened with the Barcelona 1990 or Torino 2006 Olympics or various football stadia in Italy (1990), France (1998) or Germany (2006). These are relatively straight-forward objectives, but unfortunately the results can become white elelphants and so are becoming far less popular.

There is now a shift towards competitions with more complex objectives, such as the European City of Culture a year-long celebration of a city founded by Melina Mercouri in 1985 with the European Union (EU). Initially a string of capital cities were nominated but increasingly smaller cities are getting the prize. The European Capital of Innovation launched in 2014 highlights how the EU is seeking to encourage novel approaches to city making as are awards like the Knight Cities Challenge or Bloomberg's Mayors Challenge. There are a vast number of other designations like becoming a Unesco's Creative Cities member or UN Public Innovations award winner. The European Green Capital award is new successfully won by Stockholm, Hamburg, Copenhagen and Bristol as is the World Design Capital won by both Torino and Helsinki.

All of the ambitious cities highlighted have either competed for or won a number of these competitions. [1][2][3][4]

[1] http://www.labforculture.org/en/resources-for-research/contents/research-in-focus/european-capitals-of-culture/research-mapping
[2] http://en.wikipedia.org/wiki/European_Capital_of_Culture
[3] http://knightcities.org/
[4] http://mayorschallenge.bloomberg.org/

shot approach using necessary deadlines to focus on their vision of place to force the pace for things they want to do in any case.

High quality physical environments

• There is recognition that urban quality is vital in inspiring motivation, commitment and loyalty to place.

• There is a good balance between old and new physical structures and recognition of the value of heritage and how the old can stimulate the new.

Nantes famed for its oversized elephants, but there is much more to the city.

Photograph: J.D Billaud - Nautilus

• There are rental and purchase opportunities at different price points and there are housing choices to meet different levels of income.

• Public transport and accessibility are well developed allowing for seamless connectivity and walkability and wi-fi connectivity is ubiquitous.

• An understanding of the environments and physical settings that attract young innovators.

Copenhagen was the path breaker for its 50 year strategy to recapture public space from the car starting in 1962 with "Strøget, the world's longest pedestrianized street. Barcelona's 100 pocket park scheme has been much admired. More recently Malaga and Lyons have made dramatic urban space interventions.

Perception & marketing

• Projecting a compelling story of place globally and where it is going in a sophisticated manner.

• Bringing in the media as a collaborator to communicate broader goals.

• Supporting new forms of communications including with social media strategies.

• Working on the image and perception of their city focusing on how they are contemporary and cutting edge.

Image campaigns are often contentious even successful ones like 'BeBerlin' or 'I amsterdam' or OPEN Copenhagen. These clever catch all slogans have sub-categories such as 'Be International', 'We Amsterdammers' or 'Engage with CPH' aimed at immigrants. Yet critics are concerned about people being used. Hamburg's 'Not in our Name' protest by creatives in the city is a good example as they who did not want to be associated with the creative class rhetoric of its city leaders.

Restaurant Day & Tactical Urbanism

Tactical or guerrilla urbanism describes temporary interventions in the city that seek to act as a catalyst to affect longer term change. One of the most effective is Restaurant Day started in Helsinki. The 'I love Helsinki' group were frustrated by the difficulties of setting up restaurants in the city and through social media in May 2011. 'secretely' launched what was to become a global movement 'Restaurant Day', where restaurants invade the streets, parks and courtyards. In theory it broke many rules, but it helped create a turning point in loosening up the Helsinki bureaucracy. It has grown from 45 outlets in 13 cities at the beginning to over 2000 every 3 months in 220 cities in 35 countries. This food carnival is created by thousands of people organizing and visiting one-day restaurants worldwide. The idea of the day is 'to have fun, share new food experiences and enjoy our common living environments together'.[1]

Interestingly Jussi Pajunen, the major of Helsinki noted: *Restaurant Day is exactly the sort of project that will define our future. Restaurant Day has inspired the city's population to question how things are run and to experiment and put forward new ideas of how daily life might be improved in the future.*

[1]http://www.restaurantday.org/en/info/about/

Delivering on promises

• Identifying game changers that create a new dynamic can be significant.

• Most importantly ambitious places get things done. They 'walk the talk'.

• Making invisible assets and achievements visible inspire and help develop a culture of continuous improvement and mutual learning. It provides confidence. This allows ambitious cities 'to punch above their expected weight'.

Ambition is a life force, a form of energy or engine that can help drive a city forward. It is vital to identify the right level of ambition. Not too over-ambitious to be unrealistic and not too under-ambitious so things do not move, but always ambitious nevertheless.

REFERENCES

[1] http://www.centreforcities.org/wp-content/uploads/2015/03/15-03-04-A-Century-of-Cities.pdf

[2] http://www.unesco.org/new/en/culture/themes/creativity/creative-cities-network/
https://www.youtube.com/watch?v=hkxEzSY4vys

[3] http://ec.europa.eu/programmes/creative-europe/actions/capitals-culture_en.htm

[4] http://triplehelix.stanford.edu/3helix_concept

[5] http://www.cliqproject.eu/filebank/694-Exploring_the_Quadruple_Helix_presenation.pdf

[6] http://www.ebbingekwartier.nl/

[7] http://biennaledemocrazia.it/the-project/ [8] http://www.humancities.eu/en

[9] http://www.theguardian.com/environment/2008/mar/23/freiburg.germany.greenest.city

[10] https://stad.gent/over-gent-en-het-stadsbestuur/stadsbestuur/wat-doet-het-bestuur
https://stad.gent/ghent-international/city-policy-and-structure/ghent-city-mission

[11] https://www.mannheim.de/en/shaping-city/change

[12] http://www.kirklees.gov.uk/you-kmc/deliveringServices/pdf/corporatePlan201516.pdf

[13] http://charleslandry.com/themes/creative-bureaucracy/

[14] Look up www.charleslandry.com for extensive materials on rethinking the modern bureaucracy.

[15] http://de.wikipedia.org/wiki/Still-Leben_Ruhrschnellweg

[16] http://www.citedudesign.com/fr/home/

[17] http://www.salonedelgusto.com/en/

[18] http://www.archdaily.com/390181/helsinki-central-library-winning-proposal-ala-architects

[19] http://www.iledenantes.com/en/

[20] http://www.coe.int/t/dg4/cultureheritage/culture/Cities/Default_en.asp

*Copenhagen:
looking down at
students working at
Ørestad College.*

ACKNOWLEDGEMENTS

Amongst many people interviewed in cities across Europe I especially thank the following:

Amsterdam - **Liesbeth Jansen** CEO Linkerover

Antwerp - **Phillip Heylan** Vice mayor culture and innovation, **Dirk Diels**, **Kris Achten** innovation dept.

Barcelona - **Manel San Roma** CIO Barcelona City Council

Berlin - J**ochen Sandig** Radialsystem, **Cornelia Dümcke** Culture Concepts

Bilbao - **Alfonso Martinez Cearra** Director Bilbao Metropoli 30

Bologna - **Mauro Felicori** Head of economics and promotion, **Georgia Boldrini** (ditto)

Bristol - **George Ferguson** Mayor

Copenhagen - **Flemming Borreskov** President IFHP, **Regitze Hess** COO IFHP

Dublin, **Peter Finnegan** Director economy & international relations Dublin City Council

Eindhoven - **Thom Aussen** Director Trudo, **Willie de Groot** Trudo

Flanders DC - **Pascal Cools** Director

Freiburg - **Wulf Daseking** Former head of planning

Ghent, **Karl-Filip Coenegrachts** Head of strategy and co-ordination

Grenoble - **Jean-Pierre Saez** CEO cultural observatory, ditto **Charles Ambrosino**, **Vincent Guillon**

Groningen - **Gerhard Tolner** Spatial planning, **Floor de Jong** Strategic advisor, economic affairs

Hamburg - **Jurgen Bruns-Berentelg**, Director Hafenstadt

Helsinki - **Timo Cantell** Head of urban research, **Pekka Timonen** Former director World Design Capital, **Jarmo Eskillinen** CEO Forum Virium

Kirklees - **John Heneghan** Head of strategy

Lille - **Thierry Baert** Strategy Lille Metropole, **Catherine Cullen** Former mayor for culture

Malmo - **Illmar Reepalu** Former mayor, **Christer Larsson** Head of planning

Manchester - **Sir Howard Bernstein**, CEO

Mannheim - **Rainer Kern** Director Enjoy Jazz, **Christian Hübel** Head of strategy

Nantes - **Jean-Luc Charles** SAMOA quartier de creation, **Boris Meggiorin** SAMOA **Jean Louis Bonin** Former advisor to the mayor

Ostersund - **Dag Hartman** Jamtland Regional Development, **Fia Gullickson** Jazz Kitchen

Rotterdam - **Leo Van Loon** Founder the Creative Factory, **Henk Bouwman** Transport consultant

Ruhr area - **Bernd Fesel** Head of European Centre for the Creative Economy, Dortmund

St Etienne - **Josyane Franc** Cite du Design

St Sebastian - **Euken Sese** CEO FOMENTO, **Eduardo Miera** Economics advisor

Tallinn - **Ragnar Sils**, Formerly head of cultural policy, Ministry of Culture, Estonia

Tampere - **Markku Sotaranta** University of Tampere

Torino - **Alessandro Bollo** Fitzcaraldo, **Francesco de Biase** Arts and Culture dept., **Luca Dal Pozzolo** Torino Cultural Observatory, **Luciano Pia** Architect

Umeo - **Fredrik Lindegren** Director European City of Culture

Urban specialists - **Chris Murray** Director Core Cities, **Franco Bianchini**, Prof. Leeds Beckett University, **John Worthington**, **Alan Baxter** both Academy of Urbanism, **Nick Falk**, **Phil Wood**